THE IMAGINED JUROR

The Imagined Juror

How Hypothetical Juries Influence Federal Prosecutors

Anna Offit

With a foreword by Annelise Riles

NEW YORK UNIVERSITY PRESS

New York

NEW YORK UNIVERSITY PRESS
New York
www.nyupress.org

© 2022 by New York University
All rights reserved

Chapter 2 draws on text previously published in "Prosecuting in the Shadow of the Jury," 113 *Northwestern University Law Review* 1071. It has been adapted with the permission of the Northwestern University Law Review.
Chapter 3 draws on text previously published in "With Jurors in Mind: An Ethnographic Study of Prosecutors' Narratives," *Law, Culture and the Humanities*, July 2017. It has been adapted with the permission of Sage Journals.
Chapter 4 draws on text previously published in "Race-Conscious Jury Selection," 82 *Ohio State Law Journal* 1 (2021). It has been adapted with the permission of the Ohio State Law Journal.

References to Internet websites (URLs) were accurate at the time of writing. Neither the author nor New York University Press is responsible for URLs that may have expired or changed since the manuscript was prepared.

Please contact the Library of Congress for Cataloging-in-Publication data.
ISBN: 9781479808533 (hardback)
ISBN: 9781479808540 (paperback)
ISBN: 9781479808564 (library ebook)
ISBN: 9781479808588 (consumer ebook)

New York University Press books are printed on acid-free paper, and their binding materials are chosen for strength and durability. We strive to use environmentally responsible suppliers and materials to the greatest extent possible in publishing our books.

Manufactured in the United States of America

10 9 8 7 6 5 4 3 2 1

Also available as an ebook

For Carol Greenhouse, with admiration and gratitude

CONTENTS

FOREWORD

Anna Offit's remarkable ethnography makes a pitch-perfect entrance into a political moment in which the very possibility of justice in criminal punishment has become a point of contestation. As Offit points out, the question of prosecutorial discretion—of how prosecutors make decisions, and the impact of their decisions—is now a flash point for critiques of racial bias in the criminal justice system. But if bias enters into prosecutorial thinking, how exactly do prosecutors think? As Offit points out, social scientists and legal scholars tend to reason backward, from the outcomes of prosecutors' decisions. Up to now we have lacked an internal understanding of the thought processes that lead to these unjust outcomes.

This is the first ethnographic study of US attorneys, and it is easy to see why. It took over five years for the author to gain the trust of her subjects, to negotiate access to their offices, and to conduct the painstaking interviews and participant observations that form the basis for her conclusions. The chapters that follow offer subtle and detailed analyses of particular constructions of trial narratives, jury selection processes, interactions between prosecutors and judges, and the internal conflicts and processes that mark life within a complex bureaucratic institution. This is what prosecutorial discretion actually looks like in action.

The key finding of this research—that much of the thinking of prosecutors takes place in anticipation of an imagined audience of fictional jurors—is subtle, multivalent, and yet highly consequential for the anthropology of law, the social scientific study of juries, and the legal question of how the prosecutorial system should be reformed. Offit points out that this imagined jury can serve a democratizing influence, where it forces prosecutors "to engage to some extent with alternative formulations of justice." In one of Offit's most powerful observations, she notes that juries are important not only because they deliver citizen justice but because the very possibility of citizen justice forces a different internal dialogue with imagined jurors among prosecutors. At the same time, Offit shows how limited prosecutors' imagination of jurors' experiences and thinking—often constructed through informal conversations with family members and friends—can be, and hence how the "homogeneity of a prosecutor's social milieu can thwart ethical deliberation."

Throughout the book, Offit powerfully and convincingly shows how a sophisticated ethnographic approach can contribute to the most significant legal questions of the moment. As she explains, her goal is not to indict or expose but rather to understand the lifeworld of prosecutors, to surprise us with what we think we know, taking her analytical categories and questions from what prosecutors shared with her rather than from her own a priori concerns, and also to draw out "patterns and commonalities about which they may be unaware." Offit calls this approach "illuminating justice." In a world in which our worldview is often hermetically sealed, in which evidence is consciously or unconsciously selected and interpreted to feed a priori political perspectives, this ethnographic sensibility is as refreshing as it is surprising. Readers will appreciate how much tenacity, creativity, and moral courage was required to bring forth a study of prosecutorial discretion that eschews simplistic either/or moralism and yet miraculously manages always to maintain its clear moral grounding.

I want to mention just two significant theoretical insights of this work for the anthropology of law. The first concerns the "fictional" quality of the jurors who are imagined by prosecutors. In recent years we have come to understand the power of the legal fiction as a key technique of legal analysis. We have here a different kind of fiction at the core of the law, with equally significant implications for our understanding of the workings of legal knowledge. The ethnography also contributes to our understandings of the relationship of "experts" and publics central to so much contemporary work in anthropology and social science studies. The jury is of course intended to be a purposeful lacuna in legal expertise, a point at which laypeople are explicitly given a chance to have their say. And yet we learn in this study how expert conceptions of what is a layperson, how they think, and what is justice to them influence who is chosen to participate in juries in the first place and how arguments are framed and narratives are constructed long before any actual layperson has an opportunity to engage the law. For the prosecutors Offit knew, for example, laypeople think with their "hearts" rather than their "heads," they rely on "instincts" rather than "rationalizations." They are quite explicitly the rationalist lawyer's Other.

At every point in this work, the underlying question of race and racial bias remains central. Yet what is most powerful about this study is not just the discovery of racism in prosecutorial thinking but the careful and subtle portrait that emerges of what racism actually looks, feels, and sounds like, in lived practice, among ordinary people who are neither saints nor monsters, working within a challenging institutional context full of double binds. No simple bumper sticker denunciations of prosecutors will do here. With a searing and resolute commitment to *both* anti-racism and ethnographic accountability, Offit delivers a challenging, subtle, and highly generative account—one that spurs us to face head-on the limits of our democratic institutions with open but ultimately loving eyes. For this, it is destined to become a classic in the ethnography of law.

Annelise Riles

Executive Director of the Roberta Buffett Institute for Global Studies, Associate Provost for Global Affairs, and Professor of Law at the Northwestern University Pritzker School of Law

Introduction

> Justice and injustice are not each other's opposite, as if more
> of one would mean less of the other. In these pages, justice
> is not cabined as a corrective to injustice in the world we in-
> habit in the here and now; rather, it refers to an affirmative
> refashioning of the world we live in, in some more subjunc-
> tive but still realistic temporality.
> —Carol Greenhouse, "Afterword" to *Everyday Justice*

Lay participation in the American legal system is regarded as an inviola-
ble part of the country's democratic project. After exercising one's right
to vote, serving on a jury is arguably the most direct and powerful way
to participate in our democracy.[1] Today, nearly 40 percent of American
citizens can expect to serve on a jury during their lifetimes.[2] At the same
time, trials have become infrequent and are in statistical decline—less
than 2 percent of federal criminal cases are resolved by juries today.[3] Ask
a federal prosecutor to describe an average day at work, and chances are
you will not hear about a jury trial.[4] And yet, when prosecutors describe
how they do their jobs and what their jobs mean to them, jurors seem to
be *everywhere*. It is the figure and role of this "hypothetical" or "imagined" juror in the professional lives of prosecutors that is the subject of
this book. It contends that consideration of imagined juries is crucial
at a time when social inequality, mass incarceration, and a global pandemic have prompted renewed scrutiny of how exactly laypeople do—or
do not—play an active role in criminal adjudication.

My approach is ethnographic. Drawing on my observation of a federal prosecutor's office and interviews with attorneys, I explore this par-
adoxical feature of the federal legal landscape: though laypeople only
infrequently participate in federal trials, hypothetical jurors have an
outsized presence in the decision-making and professional imagination
of some of our most powerful law enforcement officials and serve as a

critical resource to them as they attempt to make sense of ill-defined directives to seek justice and represent the United States.

How exactly? First and most concretely, prosecutors invoke hypothetical jurors when considering whether to decline or prosecute a case; whether to pursue a plea agreement; or whether to dismiss charges based on anticipated views of jurors they imagine. Here, they work together to consider how their strategies will be received, and how their arguments and framings may—or may not—resonate. In both formal meetings and informal conversations, jurors are an ever-present concern. Second, the perspectives of an imagined audience are invoked with respect to the ethical parameters and professional obligations of prosecution. Here, too, despite the relative infrequency of jury trials, federal prosecutors define their roles and the normative limits of their discretion with reference to laypeople.

This book offers an on-the-ground look at how prosecutors imagine—or invent—the jurors whose perspectives, opinions, and biases shape their approaches to trial strategy. Going further, it also examines how imagined jurors are invoked by prosecutors to navigate features of their professional lives, including office hierarchies, gendered and racial aggressions, and significant differences in opinion with respect to how cases should be prepared and presented. Alluding to the views of imagined others—the twelve people who might sit in the jury box—is a valued means of navigating the politics and practices of prosecution at the federal level. In these jurors, prosecutors find a way to talk about mercy, evolving community mores, and alternative interpretations of their cases. Through such jurors, they also develop a reflexive capacity to view *themselves* as moral actors rather than line attorneys carrying out supervisors' directives. The existence of the jury system and the possibility of facing a jury thus create a space of agency and creativity in which prosecutors negotiate conceptions of fairness, incorporate imagined citizen attributes and opinions into their work, and bring self-conscious interest in the relevance of race, class, and gender to their preparation for jury selection proceedings and trials.

Attention to the imaginative dimension of prosecutorial work is important because prosecution is, as various scholars have established, a constitutive part of a legal system that disparately investigates and punishes people of color.[5] This book will argue that understanding prosecutorial involvement in the perpetuation of institutional injustice requires attention not only to what is said and done but also to what is *not* said and done—and considered. When imagining the audience for their work, prosecutors, I discovered, rarely dwelled on the racial and socioeconomic disparities among those who were policed, investigated, incarcerated, and—critically—empaneled as jurors. Further, the prosecutors who are the focus of this study did not explicitly reflect on whether incarceration—the taken-for-granted end of most federal prosecutions—actually enhances public safety. Nor did they openly question the fairness of capital punishment during presentations and meetings where it might have felt natural to do so. Some in fact jumped at the professional opportunity to try a "death-eligible" case, as they were called.

The prosecutors I spoke with also rarely asked why there were such disparities in state and federal sentencing. Indeed, prosecutors contributed to these disparities by pursuing harsher sentences for defendants simply because they could or because they knew that arguments about aggravating factors might serve as a point of departure for off-record discussions with defense counsel. Another matter they were reticent about was the integrity of law enforcement peers with whom they worked closely. Although they might have personal reservations about their peers' moral fiber, they did not make formal complaints and often kept grievances to themselves. These silences and omissions matter.

Still, those turning to this book for an exposé of American federal prosecutors will be disappointed. My objective, as an anthropologist, is not to indict anyone for what they do or do not do. Rather, I am interested in what federal prosecutors *believe* they are doing when they prepare and argue cases, manage professional pressures, and interact with—or, more often, imagine—the laypeople who are, at least in theory, critical to the American criminal legal system. "The trick," as American anthropologist Clifford Geertz once put it, "is not to achieve some inner correspondence of spirit with your informants. . . . The trick is to figure out what the devil they think they are up to."[6] For this ethnographic study, the trick has involved working closely with federal prosecutors to develop an account of their world as they see and navigate it. It is a world, as I show, that one cannot begin to understand without grasping the central role played by the jurors who prosecutors imagine might be persuaded—or confused, offended, provoked, annoyed, bored—by the way they frame evidence, narrate events, and assign blame.

But why do assistant US attorneys talk of jurors so often when they rarely actually face juries? Federal prosecutors, I found, invoked imagined jurors and their perspectives because doing so was useful in various—and sometimes surprising—ways. For instance, mentioning jurors might help navigate office hierarchies and uncomfortable or awkward conversations. I observed that assistant US attorneys often linked opinions that were contrary to those of their supervisors to potential lay onlookers. This meant replacing "*I* disagree" with "*a juror might* disagree." In one conversation I observed, the AUSAs found themselves divided over the prosecution of a defendant who disabled online message boards that peers had used to discredit him. Some felt the defendant's actions stifled free expression, while others viewed the anonymous use of social media as a platform for bullying. Rather than personalize this source of disagreement, the prosecutors referenced imaginary jurors the trial team might face. How would *those people* view evidence along the lines they advanced? Here, invoking the jury allowed disagreeing prosecutors to reflect openly on different means of formulating their case, holding open the possibility of changing each other's minds by imagining the minds of others.

When prosecutors referred to jurors, they referred to a normative repertoire of possible responses that included ones that might lead them to decline the option to prosecute or change the way they approached the task of prosecution. Significantly, the imagined jury offered this resource without compelling a particular outcome in a given case. The figure of the jury served as a reminder that case outcomes were indeterminate, allowing prosecutors to consider a multitude of perspectives and possibilities rather than approach charging or preparation decisions based on fixed principles or rules that "prescribe particular actions in particular contexts."[7] Jurors thus presented prosecutors with a flexible vocabulary that they could use to fashion proposals that might change their colleagues' opinions.

In addition to influencing the structure and character of prosecutors' deliberations, jurors also created an opening for prosecutors to articulate ideas about justice. Jurors served as a link, or at least the aspiration of one, between the idealized lay decision maker and local conditions that gave specificity to lawyers' knowledge claims in the context of particular trials.

From the earliest stages of case preparation, the prosecutors I observed framed their intuitions about the fairness of the cases they were developing in terms of hypothetical jurors' views. A supervisor distinguished this analytic intervention from more pragmatic discussions of the sufficiency of evidence. After assessing the proof, he explained, assistant US attorneys exercised their discretion to determine whether "it was in the interest of justice" to bring charges. "If a juror is going to think who really cares that A lied to B if B did not suffer harm," he reflected, then evidence of lying might not be enough.

Consideration of jurors' perspectives also influenced the language lawyers used to characterize evidence and witnesses. An attorney who was in the process of defending the United States in a civil suit that stemmed from a plane crash, for example, felt strongly that a record of radio communications between an air traffic controller and pilot should be referred to as a "partial transcript." If the case went to trial, he reasoned, this distinction would emphasize the incompleteness of the interactions that jurors would learn about in court. It would teach hypothetical jurors, in other words, that the airplane at issue in the case was far from the sole focus of the traffic controller's attention, the presumption being that they had little personal familiarity with all the facets of an air traffic controller's job. Taking imagined jurors' experience and perspectives as a point of departure, the lawyer thus affirmed the importance of being empathetic and attentive to strategically advantageous details in choosing phrases and themes.

In the chapters that follow, prosecutorial technique is shown to be interactive, open to revision, and characterized by creative improvisation. My approach builds on anthropological studies of law that focus on legal actors' real-time practices, speech, and decision-making as they prepare cases. Attentive to variations in legal technique, such studies take into account out-of-court trial preparation, such as conversations between lawyers and their clients, and narratives that are collectively produced in the courtroom. These studies also examine lawyers' cross-examination of witnesses, including victims and experts, the role of translators in producing records of court proceedings, and the adjustments prosecutors make to their strategy in response to judges' rulings. Studies of legal technique in these contexts focus on the various discursive strategies that lawyers, litigants, and witnesses deploy during trial, highlighting their creative, impro- visational, and collaborative work.

Lawyers' and judges' questioning of litigants and witnesses in court thus offers a productive context for the study of legal technique's dynamic and contingent character. Barbara Yngvesson's analysis of interactions be- tween court clerks and laypeople in the United States exemplifies this approach in its emphasis on how these interactions facilitate the trans- formation of complaints and invention of rights. Her ethnography shows how clerks in particular courts collaboratively reframes narratives of con- flict to authorize legal intervention—leaving room for creative maneuver- ing in the process.[8] Other studies in this vein examine how prosecutorial technique can shift midtrial as well as the ways that lawyers exploit or discredit witnesses' testimony.[9] Research on immigration proceedings, too, has contributed to the study of the creativity and innovation of legal technique. Susan Bibler Coutin's study of US asylum hearings, for exam- ple, highlights judges', asylum seekers', and lawyers' reinterpretation and transformation of legal claims.[10] This research is broadly distinguished by its acceptance of the openness and uncertainty of legal processes in real time and a tendency to focus on how trials are conducted and the kinds of strategies used rather than on their outcomes.[11] Anthropologists and ethnographic legal scholars' conceptions of narratives as flexible, nego- tiable products of a dialogic process are another helpful analogue to the process of knowledge production discussed in this book.[12]

For instance, insofar as assistant US attorneys' silence revealed com- placency with a status quo that replicated inequity, this finding supports the insights of scholars who have drawn attention to a broader tendency among prosecutors to adopt consciously "color-blind" orientations to- ward their work that mask systemic injustices. In her ethnographic re- search on the courtroom work group in Cook County, Chicago, Nicole Gonzalez Van Cleve refers to this phenomenon as "colorblind racism"— characterized by its tacit reinforcement of the "moral integrity and race neutrality of prosecutors' work."[13] While the prosecutors Van Cleve inter- viewed acknowledged racial disparities among defendants and victims, they had difficulty identifying the source of these disparities and tended to identify their own bias as "unconscious and unintentional."[14] Though state prosecutors are the focus of Van Cleve's analysis, her observations capture the tendency of the assistant US attorneys in this study to more readily identify racist practices *outside* their office, on the part of law enforcement agents with whom they worked (for example), while rarely acknowledging the racial valence of their own assumptions about the material circumstances and perspectives of defendants. Because this study seeks to uncover the "constraints and conditions" under which federal prosecutors work, its findings can be read alongside those that have shed light on routinized expressions of prejudice and bias among lawyers.[15]

Prosecutors' silence on such issues may reflect the fact that the legal landscape in which they work serves them well; many of those I spoke with acknowledged that they were better compensated than their state counterparts. These prosecutors could also perhaps turn a blind eye to the racial segregation and heavy law enforcement presence in the neighborhoods surrounding the office by choosing not to travel through them as part of their own commutes from more affluent neighborhoods where they resided.

Though the federal prosecutors I interviewed were predominantly male (63 percent), 22 percent of my interlocutors were people of color, indicating that racial hierarchies in society can be supported by lay and professional legal actors of all backgrounds.[16] Defendants in corruption, fraud, and other white-collar prosecutions were often white, affluent community leaders whom prosecutors tended to describe as individuals who should "know better" than to exploit the trust of their constituents. Sex crimes against women and children were also typically perpetrated by white defendants, including educators, businessmen, and others with access to power who profited from their coercive behavior.

The racial divide that empirical legal scholars have noted was most starkly apparent during my study of narcotics prosecutions, those charged under the Racketeer Influenced and Corrupt Organizations (RICO) Act, and in gun possession cases. No prosecutor I spoke with ever commented on the disproportionate presence of Black defendants or victims in their cases. They did not comment on the disparate number of Black citizens represented in federal building and courthouse security lines—presenting what Van Cleve refers to as a "racialized courtroom landscape" reflecting a demographic disconnect between subjects of the criminal justice system—including witnesses and family members who arrived as spectators—and the suited lawyers who arrived to do their jobs.[17]

The prosecutors I observed also refrained from questioning the limits of their capacity to anticipate jurors' views or recognize the socioeconomic and racial exclusion inherent to the process by which laypeople are summoned to court. No doubt the *types* of jurors prosecutors imagine naturally affect the way they think their cases might be judged. If a juror is envisioned as being a perceptive and evenhanded actor, for example, a prosecutor might be more inclined to critically evaluate investigative practices with this juror in mind. If a juror is envisioned as being ignorant and inattentive, on the other hand, prosecutors might take a less reflexive approach to their work.[18]

The hypothetical jurors who emerge in prosecutors' accounts and conversations are members of a generative audience. They are imagined to have idiosyncratic backgrounds and biases and firm intuitions about the fairness and shortcomings of the law. It is also the case that such jurors do not reflect the demographically diverse population that would in reality be summoned to court. They are, for example, often presumed to be law-abiding, deferential to law enforcement agents, and fearful of criminal activity that might affect the perceived safety of their communities or the value of their property. They are envisioned as being employed or retired and living comfortably from savings and as traveling to the courthouse in cars they own from houses they own and to have access to the internet and social media. In practice, as discussed in chapter 4, when prosecutors imagined prospective jurors of color or those who were poor, such jurors assumed flattened and generalized attributes. They were often referred to as if they represented homogenous groups. For example, I observed prosecutors actively refrain from using peremptory strikes against Black jurors and encourage use of cause challenges against jurors who were poor out of concern about the discriminatory or insensitive implications of each decision, respectively.

Where a number of anthropological studies of legal technique and narrative center on discrete hearings in relation to an already known outcome, this book focuses on pre-verdict settings in which case outcomes are unknown, shifting the analytical burden toward interpretive premises rather than strategic efficacy. Significantly, in focusing on lawyers' everyday work, my research builds on scholarship that unsettles rigid distinctions between lay and professional legal knowledge.[19] It demonstrates that commonsense intuitions about fairness are central to legal technique. And further, extralegal conceptions of justice and ideas regarding legal discretion are interdependent rather than discrete and autonomous knowledge repertoires. In the course of interacting with colleagues and other law enforcement agents, prosecutors routinely brought such extralegal notions of justice into their case assessments and office talk.

Research Process

The focus of this study is a group of assistant US attorneys who referred to themselves interchangeably as "federal prosecutors" and "AUSAs." Despite the significant role they play in the American criminal legal system, federal prosecutors have seldom been the subject of qualitative empirical research. Although this has begun to change, one of the greatest hurdles to engaging in long-term qualitative studies of prosecutors remains the strict limitations placed on access.[20] Members of the public routinely enter US attorney's offices as part of the formal process of contributing to or being the subject of a case, but prosecutors do not otherwise make themselves available to anyone who might be interested in discussing their work. Instead, public affairs or media contacts assume that role, ensuring that all messaging is vetted and carefully phrased.

This makes the current study—involving a half decade of on-the-ground, in-the-office ethnographic research—very unusual and, I would like to think, valuable. The practical and logistical barriers to access were still daunting even with the invitation I received to conduct research from the US attorney's office.[21] How would the Department of Justice facilitate the uncompensated entry of a researcher? First, and before I could enter the office, I underwent a compulsory background check. I listed every place I had lived and worked for the past seven years and provided the contact information of people who could confirm the accuracy of that information. The next barrier to entry was a physical one; in order to visit the federal building without waiting in a visitor's line and having to run my belongings through an X-ray machine, step through a metal detector, and receive an adhesive visitor badge every day, I needed a photo ID card to show security guards. And to access the building's interior corridors, conference rooms, and offices of the prosecutors I met with, I was given a separate key card and passcode. The final barrier was social. As a cultural anthropologist, even a legally

trained one, I was a stranger with strange goals. I was not there to prepare cases, but rather to learn how my interlocutors thought one should
prepare cases. I was not there seeking professional advancement—or
compensation—but was interested in how my interlocutors managed
their intraoffice relationships and sought to build their careers while
"doing justice." In the process of "being there," I made friends, attended
retirement parties and baby showers, went bowling, visited homes, invited people to my home, introduced families, shared gossip, swapped
career advice, and offered consolation. I also accepted an assignment
in the office to develop a synoptic overview of judges' approaches to
voir dire, as well as an invitation to share the insights from this side
project as part of a training for the AUSAs before I departed the office.[22]
In short, this was not a one-way exchange. Anthropological research
of this sort is personal and inevitably involves building relationships
of mutual vulnerability, trust, and understanding. It is undergirded by
the ethical principle, enshrined by the American Anthropological Association, to expand the horizons of our collective understanding while
doing no harm to the interlocutors who make that expansion possible.

During the first months of fieldwork, I interviewed 133 criminal and
civil division assistant US attorneys in the office for the first time, which
established a foundation for countless and more informal conversations
in the coming years.[23] Quotations from interviewees included in the book
have been anonymized to convey generalized reflections about decision-
making processes. Some conversations took place in prosecutors' offices
during lunch or coffee breaks, and others lasted for multiple hours, broken
up over several days. I spoke with prosecutors who had varying levels of
trial experience and who worked in both the criminal and civil divisions
of the office. Some prosecutors had never tried a case in their careers, and
others were in the midst of trials when I spoke with them.

To protect their privacy, I randomly assigned a two-letter code to each
interviewee (e.g., AA, AB, AC), and in this book I omit details that might
identify an individual, a case, or the office's location to readers outside
the office. The reflections that were shared with me within the context of
the research are completely anonymized and often decontextualized for
further protection. Due to the nature of this subject matter, and out of
an abundance of caution, this level of anonymization goes beyond that
which is required by an institutional review board. While some readers

might feel that the shedding of this kind of empirical detail detracts from the narrative richness of the ethnography, I would contend that such measures are critical for the protection of people who offered a rare and candid look at the world of federal prosecution.

Although this book builds on recent accounts of how hypothetical profiles generated by prosecutors are inextricably bound to decision-making processes in the criminal context, it is unique in its long-term qualitative engagement with a group of lawyers who exercise discretion in a manner that is largely inaccessible and invisible to the American public they purportedly serve.[24] No anthropologist, to my knowledge, has ever gained access to a US attorney's office as a research site. Yet the value of ethnographic research in the legal realm has not been lost on the discipline, which has long asserted its critical contribution of attention to the state actors and institutions empowered to influence the lives of ordinary people. Laura Nader, for example, argues that the functioning of a democracy is contingent on citizens' "access to decision-makers" and "institutions of government," which requires such citizens to "know something about the major institutions, government or otherwise, that affect their lives."[25] Drawing on the work of critical legal theorists and new legal realists, ethnographers of global institutions have also highlighted the value of research attentive to the "everyday experience of those who participate in legal processes."[26] As some of the most powerful and least transparent law enforcement officials in the legal system, federal prosecutors have much to teach us about how justice is formulated when no one is watching. This knowledge, in turn, can be democratized, an important step at a time when prosecutorial ethics is a source of debate and proposed reform.

At the prosecutor's office, as I collected extensive data on jury selection practices, I came to be perceived as an in-house expert on voir dire strategy. For this reason, some prosecutors chose to incorporate me—well aware of my status as a researcher—into their case preparation and jury selection practices. With these trial teams, I participated in trial strategy meetings, observed and sometimes assisted with witness preparation sessions, helped revise exhibits, contributed to discussions related to opening and closing statements, and researched legal issues. In some cases, the sociality of strategy discussions and planning sessions followed quieter weeks of work, like contributing to the aspects of jury selection that leave one "covered in paper-cuts and exhausted"—as Bruno Latour described his own foray into researching legal professionals at the Conseil d'État in France.[27] Participating in jury selection, for example, could require reading, labeling, piling, sorting, stacking, annotating, and physically transporting thousands of pages of questionnaires. As prosecutors (and I) compiled lists of jurors to revisit with follow-up questions—or to excuse from the process altogether—we assigned the questionnaire packets numbers so multiple copies could simultaneously be read (sometimes aloud), highlighted, double-checked, or recopied. Questionnaire packets for jurors could range from ten to more than a hundred questions.

In theory, at least, jury selection proceedings are open to the public. Because prospective jurors occupied benches that would otherwise be reserved for onlookers or reporters, I often sat in seats designated for case agents or at counsel's table. I was also granted permission by judges—with the consent of defense counsel—to sit or stand within earshot of conversations with jurors at sidebar. I tried to be attentive to the minutiae of my interlocutors' decision-making. This turned out to be a mutually advantageous arrangement. I was as eager to make sense of prosecutors' observations, reflections, and deliberations as many of them were to elicit insight from a "more objective," outside party. But both in and outside of the office, this role had ethical implications, as judges and defense attorneys assumed that my work contributed to prosecutors' cases. This real and presumed alignment of interests had consequences that affected the depth and scope of my fieldwork. It meant that prosecutors spoke with me candidly, while defense attorneys and other court personnel kept their distance. It also presented me with the challenge of maintaining critical distance from my interlocutors' perceptions of their work and jobs. Though I was clearly marked as a researcher and nonemployee, I was also treated like a confidant, as prosecutors shared accounts of harassment, discrimination, or past contributions to the wrongful prosecution of an innocent person who was later exonerated— among other difficult experiences.

Most of the trial preparation I participated in took place in the US attorney's office, not far from the courthouse. Though research and writing were solitary endeavors, case preparation was punctuated by continual interruptions. This included flurries of emails exchanged among supervisors, appellate division attorneys, and assistants. It also included communications from judges' deputies, phone calls from defense attorneys, and messages from case agents concerned about witness logistics. Prosecutors often stopped by colleagues' or supervisors' offices to share frustrations from the day or to informally seek advice. Some of these conversations took place during coffee runs. Infrequent though they were, trials commanded attention. As they wheeled bags of binders and notepads to and from courtrooms, trial teams could be heard chatting about interminable cross-examinations, insufferable adversaries, poorly conceived defense motions, and nights of work that lay ahead. And during midday breaks, trial issues took precedence over supervisors' other work.

Participant observation was well-suited to the study of prosecutorial strategy and ethics, as prosecutors' decision-making in advance of—and during—trial was informed by their continuous interaction. I often served as a sounding board as prosecutors prepared to bring their ideas to peers. Sometimes prosecutors wanted to incorporate my suggestions into their opening and closing statements and cross-examinations, in which case I elaborated on and refined ideas in conversation with them. Prosecutors were also presented with opportunities for reflection as they interacted with others who offered conflicting views—including supervisors, colleagues, case agents, and witnesses. Disagreement in these contexts offered a window into how prosecutors understood, formulated, and changed their opinions.

In sum, this ethnography of federal prosecutors is based on data that bears the impression of my particular experience, perspective, and intermittent involvement in the very work that interests me as a researcher. Those unfamiliar with cultural anthropological research might argue that the present study is thus biased or tainted. This, however, would misapprehend the nature of this distinctive social science, which pays as its cost the mediation of its data by the personal circumstances of the ethnographer for the benefit of building accounts, if only incompletely, of the unique lifeworlds of other kinds of people. The circumstances that produced my insights about the centrality and utility of imagined jurors are unique and unlikely to be replicated. At the same time, the insights themselves are linked to structural features of the day-to-day work of federal prosecutors in the contemporary United States, and thus I am confident that they would be surfaced in large part by a different study, in a different office or offices. For this reason, I consider my empirical generalizations to be of significance beyond the present case.

Overview of Book

The chapters that follow develop three themes. The first is the relevance of imagined jurors to nearly every aspect of prosecutorial work. The second is that grappling with the perspectives of these hypothetical others prompts ethical reflections that are critical to how prosecutors understand the right and wrong, good and bad of that work. The third and final theme is that race, class, gender, and other categories of identity figure in the prosecutorial imaginary in very limited ways, suggesting the need to enhance antidiscrimination law. These themes emerge and are elaborated within and across the book's six chapters.

Chapter 1 examines the federal prosecutor's role in the criminal justice system, focusing on this role's legal underpinnings and ambiguities. In particular, I consider how prosecutors turn to hypothetical jurors for prosecutors as they navigate their professional and ethical obligation to see that justice is done.

Chapter 2 continues this discussion, arguing that prosecutors deploy imagined jurors to assess the merits of their cases—including the quality of investigative techniques and credibility of witnesses—during every phase of case preparation. An effect of lawyers' continual reference to imagined jurors is their explicit incorporation of what they perceive to be local knowledge and commonsense ideas about fairness into their decision-making processes. Though I found that this lay knowledge was rarely generated through firsthand encounters with actual jurors, it nevertheless animated the formal and informal case evaluations and strategy meetings of AUSAs.

Building on the first two chapters' attention to prosecutorial ethics, chapters 3 and 4 focus on the imaginative labor prosecutors devote to making sense of—and trying to effectuate—their duty to serve as officers of the court rather than as zealous advocates. In practice, as we see in the context of preparation for opening and closing statements and jury selection proceedings, the performance of this impartial persona requires collaborative narrative work. Chapter 3 explores the processes by which prosecutors develop and revise opening and closing statements for trial. The first section of the chapter shows that these accounts are keyed to perspectives that prosecutors attribute to hypothetical jurors. The second section focuses on particular narrative techniques and prosecutors' perceptions of their suitability for informing jurors' assessments of character and evidence.

Chapter 4 turns to a discussion of how prosecutors invoke hypothetical jurors in preparation for the potential empanelment of actual jurors. Even when prosecutors were given the rare opportunity to directly interact with lay decision makers during jury selection proceedings, jurors remained elusive and unpredictable. This was also true of the people lawyers questioned in court, since federal prosecutors in the district could not interact with jurors postverdict. A vital function of the lawyers' assessments of prospective jurors during their empanelment, the chapter argues, was the opening it created for prosecutors to again explicitly define and assert the parameters of their own professional and ethical identities. For example, some self-consciously tried to identify and empanel Black prospective jurors so as not to be perceived as racist. They also advocated for excusing prospective jurors with claims of financial hardship in an effort to be perceived as benevolent and generous toward citizens whose occupations or attitudes suggested jury service would be burdensome. In both cases, prosecutors' strategic considerations were paired with—if not supplanted by—an explicit focus on how their rationales for empaneling or dismissing potential jurors might reflect on others' perceptions of *them*.

The book's last two chapters—chapters 5 and 6—take illustrative criminal prosecutions as points of departure for thinking about the relationship between hypothetical jurors and the formulation of justice by prosecutors and judges. Chapter 5 examines the role that hypothetical jurors played as the prosecutors I observed engaged in the narrative work central to distinguishing defendants and witnesses who are credible from those who are not. This distinction is crucial to the enforcement of evidentiary rules that permit witnesses to be impeached on the basis of having an untruthful character. For the prosecutors in the office, though, character scrutiny begins with the jury selection process and often extends beyond the question of whether a layperson should be taken at her word in responding to voir dire questions. I focus on cases in which prosecutors work collectively to frame both jurors and, later, witnesses as liars to demonstrate that character judgment, and stereotyping are central to this enterprise. In the case of character assessments of witnesses, jurors remain the implicit referents of prosecutors' strategic attempts to construct liars through carefully crafted lines of questioning.

Finally, chapter 6 offers an example of the role that hypothetical jurors play for another critical legal actor: the district court judge. Drawing at length on one case I observed, I examine a judge's elaboration of hypothetical jurors' perspectives when applying a discretionary rule of evidence (FRE 403). This rule considers whether the probative value of relevant evidence is significantly outweighed by its potential to unfairly prejudice jurors. Though real jurors adjudicated the case, the judge relied on their own imagined jurors to dramatically change the course of the trial. As part of this exercise, the prosecutors in the case came to appreciate that competing visions of justice can be claimed in an imagined jury's name and caught a glimpse of what justice in the shadow of a judge, rather than a jury, might look like.

Taken together, these chapters tell the story of how some of the most powerful professional legal actors in America make sense of—and pursue—justice with reference to an imagined audience of laypeople. This story, I believe, captures the dynamic, creative, and contingent character of prosecutorial work and ethics. The book concludes by drawing attention to the jury system's current crisis of legitimacy, and the issues that stem from prosecutors' engagement with imagined jurors who think like and resemble them, rather than a diversely constituted and representative public. I argue that the American jury system can only democratize our legal system if its juries—both real and imagined—reflect the full range of identities and perspectives of our communities. The disappearance of juries would not only deprive defendants of the opportunity to be tried by their peers but also deny prosecutors a vital resource with which to imagine perspectives on their cases that exceed their own life experiences. It is this vantage point that permits prosecutors to expand the range of considerations that inform their cases—and it is a vantage point that must be broadened in an era of mass incarceration and the prioritization of prosecutions that exacerbate social inequality.

1

Prosecutorial Discretion

The prosecutor is the gatekeeper of the system, the one who decides which cases go from the paddy wagon to the courtroom. The prosecutor's conscience is the invisible guardian of our rights, just as the defense lawyer is the visible guardian.
—David Luban, "The Conscience of a Prosecutor"

On a late Monday afternoon, I knocked on a half-open office door and took a seat across from an AUSA. They seemed relieved to have company, though they were not looking for small talk. Instead, this AUSA immediately launched into a meandering account of a case that they found uniquely vexing. It was the same case that we chatted about every few weeks, when I stopped by. The defendant was a dynamic, popular, and outspoken member of the community. What nagged at the AUSA was this: the law enforcement agents who investigated and ultimately arrested him were white, and the AUSA was white. The defendant was Black. The AUSA did not want to pursue the case, but it was an assignment. And even in relatively senior position in the office, they did not think they had a choice—well, short of quitting.

The AUSA's anxiety was palpable. There were other times when this person said they "rued the day" a law enforcement agent brought this defendant to their supervisor's attention. In fact, the FBI had originally been monitoring someone else in connection with a bigger case. The outspoken community member was linked to this case but was supposed to "flip" to aid the investigation in exchange for assurance that the US attorney's office would treat him leniently. But he refused to cooperate. He denied committing crimes and was confident a jury would acquit him.

The anxious AUSA indicated that under different circumstances, the US attorney's office might have declined to prosecute this kind of case. I asked what made the case so challenging and what types of considerations might have figured in a decision not to charge the man in the first place. The AUSA said that racial tensions and inequities were central concerns. National attention at the time was focused on high-profile police killings of unarmed Black men. And a wave of Black Lives Matter protests had gained momentum and attention across the country.

If the case went to trial, the defendant planned to accuse the government of entrapment. In his view, this was just another example of law enforcement depriving him of opportunities to earn a living and find social support. Early in life, he faced several criminal convictions, which he attributed to the overpolicing of his poor neighborhood. The AUSA believed this defense might actually resonate with prospective jurors who shared the view that police were also "terrorizing" their communities. And, once again, it would not help, the AUSA continued, that everyone on the government's side was white—case agents, confidential informants, and the trial team.

This was one of few moments during my fieldwork when a prosecutor spontaneously commented on the impact of racism and disparate policing on a case. And though this AUSA thought the evidence against the defendant clearly met the office's legal threshold for prosecution, it was not the type of investigation that many federal prosecutors would have felt compelled to pursue. It was a matter of discretion. This critical distinction between a legally and ethically defensible prosecution brought the power of the office and prosecutor into relief.

According to the Department of Justice's *Justice Manual*, the "wide latitude" that federal prosecutors have to determine "when, whom, how, and even whether" to prosecute is a central feature of their jobs.[1] In 2016, federal prosecutors reportedly declined to prosecute 16.4 percent of cases that came before them—a figure that excludes the numerous ongoing or incomplete investigations that FBI agents usually bring to the attention of line attorneys informally.[2] This precharging phase of casework is conducted in secret. The public has no ability to assess the strength of evidence as it is gathered, the severity of the crimes that a prosecutor will consider charging, or the prosecution's theory of a case. All of this develops within the space created by the prosecutor's "wide latitude."

The absence of public disclosure of declination decisions means that it is typically unclear whether prosecutors' offices have consistent procedures in place to analyze or help guide their decisions. Further, we know little about what determines the selection of particular investigative techniques, the inclusion of evidence, or the final decision to pursue formal charges rather than decline, dismiss, or refer a case elsewhere. Prosecutors themselves are unlikely to know much about this either: a study of 158 state prosecutor's offices, for example, revealed that as many as one-third of offices collected *no data* on case declinations or dismissals.[3]

This lack of information, as well as the denial of public access to information that exists, has been subject to critique by legal scholars concerned that prosecutors exercise discretion with limited oversight.[4] And the absence of written or uniformly communicated guidance on factors that should influence charging or declination decisions has consequences *within* the prosecutors' office, too. Federal prosecutors seeking parameters for these types of decisions from the *Justice Manual* will find little guidance. Grounds for recommending prosecution, according to this document, extend beyond the question of whether a prosecutor believes that a defendant's conduct constitutes a federal crime or whether admissible evidence could achieve a guilty verdict at trial. These are necessary but not sufficient conditions. A prosecutor could still decide to decline to prosecute a case if she believed, for example, that moving forward would fail to satisfy a "substantial federal interest."[5]

Though the *Justice Manual* does not offer case-specific recommendations as to when the prosecution of a crime might serve this kind of "substantial interest," it does direct federal prosecutors to assess the strength of their cases and evidence with reference to likely jury trial outcomes, specifically, with reference to the likelihood of a guilty verdict by an unbiased jury. The *Manual* also mentions a circumstance in which prosecutors should *not* let anticipated juror perceptions influence their judgment: when some aspect of the case is perceived as being "*un*popular" or a defendant is "overwhelming[ly] popular," a prosecutor can still properly conclude that prosecution is appropriate.[6]

A subsequent section of the *Manual* outlines considerations that are relevant to prosecutors' declination decisions, including the "nature and seriousness of the offense," which is afforded the greatest elaboration.[7] Though the comment reiterates that the prosecutor has an ethical imperative to not decline a case solely on the grounds that it might be "a particularly unpopular case," it also invites scrutiny of the *public's* likely perception of a prosecution. The prosecutor should, the *Manual* explains, carefully consider the public's possible indifference to, interest in, or opposition to the case, as well as the public's possible conclusion that the crime in question is "technical or relatively inconsequential" or that it is a "minor matter of private concern."

But how should a prosecutor conceptualize this so-called public perception of a prosecution in the narrow factual context of a particular case? Who constitutes this public? People who share geographic proximity to the relevant events? Victims? Those sympathetic to defendants? This book reveals that prosecutors do constantly make reference to this ill-defined public through conceiving of a make-believe audience for their work that I variously call the "imagined" or "hypothetical" jury. These juries, though they exist only in the minds of the prosecutors, are very real with respect to their impact on prosecutorial decision-making. They are endowed with attributes and opinions, and are invoked to consider critically everything from the merits of evidence and ethics of investigative techniques to the credibility of a witness and the persuasiveness of opening and closing statements.

Federal prosecutors' regular practice of not only considering but in fact actively *creating* and integrating the vantage points of hypothetical lay decision-makers into their conversations and discretionary judgment is particularly notable at a time when juries resolve a small fraction of federal criminal and civil cases. It is also a practice that invites caution on a number of fronts. One might question, as a preliminary matter, whether prosecutors should be in the business of deferring difficult ethical decisions, even rhetorically, to imagined others. There is also the issue of *how* prosecutors imagine jurors, and the consequences of this considered (or more visceral) judgment. Prosecutors who impute biases and other preconceived notions to those who might serve as the arbiters of their cases may be less inclined to bring charges against suspected perpetrators of crimes against victims perceived as incredible or unpopular. The same is true of prosecutors who presume that jurors share characteristics in common with them, including stable employment, respect for law enforcement, and high school or college degrees. To the extent that scholars have brought to light prosecutors' disparate approaches to charging cases of sexual assault and police misconduct,[8] future research might reveal that prosecutors in such cases presume that hypothetical jurors view the accusers in such cases as unworthy or imperfect victims.

Invocations of the imagined "reasonable juror," like the "reasonable man" in criminal law, may thus serve as a self-interested rationale for selectively prosecuting cases involving victims with whom prosecutors sympathize or can relate to.[9] Since prosecutors cannot know what a jury will collectively *do* in a given case until confronted with a real jury, and because jurors remain unknowable to prosecutors even after they are empaneled, hypothetical jurors create an opening for the machinations of privileged and powerful legal actors to authorize expedient, self-interested, or prejudicial case decisions.

By the same token, and to the extent that prosecutors imagine juries as diversely constituted by individuals with varying and unpredictable sympathies, hypothetical jurors may introduce a tempering and humanizing effect on their work. It is possible, in other words, that imagined jurors bring to prosecutors' decisions a mitigating influence that draws on the way they conceive of a broader community's voice.

The malleability of the imagined juror can therefore be understood as a weakness or strength of the American criminal legal system, depending on one's vantage point and aims. And to an extent, this opening for subjective judgment is an inherent feature of trial procedure and evidentiary rules. Judges imagine jurors as determining the bounds of relevance for evidence that will be seen or heard at trial.[10] They make a similar determination in considering the merits of a Rule 29 motion for a judgment of acquittal at the conclusion of the government's case in considering whether an imagined jury can reasonably convict a defendant.[11] These are critical decisions, all made and justified with reference to how professional legal actors *believe* the public might respond.

Conclusions about the role of hypothetical jurors based on a one-office study—for example, this book—cannot easily be generalized. Moreover, it is not a given that findings derived from research conducted in the 2010s still hold even at this particular site: after all, the personnel of a US attorney's office is transient, evolving as people pursue their careers and new political administrations bring renewal and rearrangement of personnel and office leaders. The US attorney's office that is the focus of this book is, for all practical purposes, not an office that exists today in the form in which I found it. It is an office with a dynamic and distinctive culture, shaped by the voices of those who shared cases, hallways, war rooms, and war stories about the successes and disappointments of their jobs.

And yet, I would contend that my insights about the remarkable place of the hypothetical jury hold—both for this office and for US attorney's offices in general. The reason is simple: these jurors' influence is a reflection of their usefulness for solving everyday problems encountered by AUSAs, and these problems stem from structural features of an American criminal legal system that provides federal prosecutors with wide discretion, little guidance, and the vague expectation that at some point they *might* actually have to face—and persuade—twelve members of the public. Another reason I suspect that imagined jurors are significant more generally is because of where they emerge—that is, in talk. The prosecutors I observed weighed the merits of decisions by discussing their cases with one another (and, as it turned out, with me). In these conversations, the appearance of an imagined juror or jury was never a surprise.

Speaking of Discretion

The anxious AUSA's account of the factors that militated against prosecuting the outspoken member of the community would be invisible to anyone outside the prosecutor's office—they were not memorialized in any memo or shared with any judge. Prosecutorial discretion, as I observed it, was inherently dynamic and variable and found direction through interactions with peers. Prosecutors did not experience their discretion as an abstract power—or as a power at all, as unit supervisors had an editorial hand in everything from grand jury presentations to the wording of charging documents. As a practical and empirical matter, the study of prosecutorial discretion is a study of what prosecutors say to one another and to those they work with outside the office about their jobs in both formal and informal capacities. It is a study of lawyers' talk, whether in the form of casual conversations or rehearsed narratives delivered at moot meetings or in court. Although prosecutorial decision-making is not a subject that has been taken up by linguistic and cultural anthropologists, this project builds on the pioneering work of those who place legal actors' language use at the forefront of their inquiries into legal processes and institutions.

Anthropological approaches to legal language document the tension between the real-time indeterminacy of lawyers' talk and the static formality of legal opinions and written memos. They emphasize the often improvised character of such talk.[12] Legal language, by these accounts, emerges as a medium for different possible arguments and outcomes.[13] Austin Sarat and William Felstiner's analysis of divorce lawyers' talk illustrates this approach. They show how multiple discursive strategies, including invocations of formalist, equitable, and realistic conceptions of law, inform the interpretive frames divorce lawyers present to their clients to help them make legal decisions.[14] Other approaches to legal language, to which this study contributes, set aside consideration of legal outcomes altogether, focusing instead on the uncertainty of verdicts.[15]

In this book, I focus on prosecutors' work as they understand and articulate it, while drawing out patterns and commonalities about which they may be unaware. This approach to illuminating justice exemplifies the capacity of ethnographic research to build legal knowledge and contribute to legal theory from the ground up.[16] Ethnography is an immersive and qualitative research method that draws attention to the mundane circumstances of everyday work and life, offering a "detailed, up-close investigation of both the subjective and objective aspects of cultural life," including how people individually and subjectively make sense of their roles within a community.[17] The analytic priorities of this book thus emerge from the reflections and practices of my research subjects rather than a source external to them.[18] Rather than focus on the ends and outcomes of prosecutors' labor, it is attuned to the social and practical contexts in which they articulate and understand the principles that guide their work toward those ends.

Unlike critiques that focus on the theoretical limits of the discretion of prosecutors as compared with that of other institutional actors, this book examines the how and why of everyday prosecutorial work—*from the perspective of prosecutors.*

The empirical question of how federal prosecutors engage in discretionary and nontransparent decision-making and what kind of role they invent for jurors in this process is one that cannot readily be answered by surveys, interviews, or even in-court observation alone. The reason is obvious: lawyers' assertions about what they do can differ dramatically from what they in fact do, as evidenced by spontaneous and unselfconscious comments and conversations with peers and supervisors.[19] Participant observation allows a researcher to ensure that prosecutors' responses to questions, while undoubtedly useful, are not taken at face value but instead are compared to the actual, real-time decision-making processes and impromptu practices that characterize these prosecutors' work.

And what of *justice*—that critical value that is said to emerge from this work? Though the Supreme Court has argued that the prosecutor represents "not an ordinary party to a controversy" but rather "a sovereignty" who has an interest in seeing that "justice shall be done," the question of what justice *means* to different prosecutors in the context of different cases, offices, and organizational environments has largely gone unexamined by social scientists and legal scholars, in large part owing to impediments to access faced by researchers seeking to engage in long-term participant observation alongside them.[20] What has been available are the handful of firsthand accounts published by former federal prosecutors. Preet Bharara, for example, the former US attorney of the Southern District of New York, recalls that prosecutors had ample room for ethical interpretation and that therefore one should view the "rule-of-law mantra" with a grain of salt, as it can conceal a delicate "judgment call, a value-based decision, or some other policy position." In his view, failing to acknowledge this room for maneuver is itself an abdication of the responsibility to carefully deliberate about courses of action that have consequences for a person's life.[21]

Recall, however, that without being able to read these kinds of reflections against the everyday work of federal prosecution, it is difficult to say whether such stated conceptions are actually relevant with respect to how AUSAs do their jobs. Such gaps in knowledge only reinforce the importance of studying prosecutors' offices ethnographically.

Prosecutorial Power

Though prosecutors are afforded discretion at most stages of casework, its first exercise typically comes with the decision to indict or *decline* to indict a defendant. The significance of this discretion warrants emphasis, since federal prosecution can have deeply punitive and lasting consequences for the ordinary people who find themselves transformed into targets of investigations or, later, into criminal defendants.[22] Even a misdemeanor conviction can turn a person into a legal subject encumbered by debt and subject to interminable monitoring, civic exclusion, and potential carceral sentences. The potential for these consequences is created the moment a prosecutor decides an investigation or arrest should become a criminal charge.[23]

Prosecutors' power to choose *not* to prosecute cases thus also has an important institutional role, as it serves as a check on policing decisions. As Alexandra Natapoff explains, declinations are

> a particularly crucial mechanism for ensuring that criminal cases are only brought when they are well founded, fair, and in the public interest. They are the reason why getting arrested is not the same thing as being charged with a crime, and they give meaning to the all-important boundary between the policing function and the adversarial legal system.[24]

In the misdemeanor context, for example, prosecutors may fail to appropriately screen cases for a host of reasons, including lack of experience. That can result in police officers wielding "de facto prosecutorial power."[25] Having more resources at its disposal than state law enforcement offices, the federal system—at the figurative top of the pyramid—is presumably also better positioned to take a more cautious and discerning approach to cases it considers for prosecution.[26] But much depends on the culture of an office, which can be set and altered by those at the top who allocate material and personnel resources to reflect different personal approaches to incentivizing types of work and distinct political priorities.

The US attorneys who head each office are appointed by the president and confirmed by the US Senate. The US attorney for the office I spent time in arrived with a particular agenda for how the office should be reorganized. This agenda affected which attorneys would be promoted to supervisory positions and which units within the office would be expanded or eliminated, based on priorities set by the Department of Justice. It also reflected this US attorney's personal impressions of—and relationships with—those within the office, as well as others who were hired based on relationships outside the office. This reorganization had implications for line attorneys' decision-making processes, as it dictated who each attorney would need to consult for feedback and approval.

US attorneys could also set the tone for how they expected line attorneys to evaluate their own work. They might encourage prosecutors to focus on making case decisions grounded in "justice" or, alternatively, based on the likelihood and swiftness of a guilty verdict. Upon the departure of the US attorney in place at the time of my research and as my own project came to an end, I heard attorneys comment on the fact that new office leadership measured office productivity by the number of criminal cases prosecuted by the office. Professional accomplishment, by this logic, was quantified as the number of cases the office charged during the new US attorney's tenure—a number that was reported in public messaging that announced organizational changes.[27] Missing from this metric for progress was any account or acknowledgment of the cases not pursued by the office, which were erased through their omission.

The discretion exercised by both state and federal prosecutors has spurred calls for reform. Ideas that have been advanced include instituting legislative checks on prosecutors' decision-making power, electing (state) prosecutors willing to implement reforms, and undertaking a broader rethinking of a public prosecution system that permits prosecutors to see what most people would view as "victimless crimes" as causing societal harm that requires formal redress.[28] Other reform suggestions include encouraging prosecutors to use their discretion to outmaneuver unjust laws or policies, such as by working to avoid the automatic triggers for mandatory minimums that contribute to onerous and disparate prison sentences.[29]

Others question the wisdom of conferring prosecutors with so much power and discretion in the first place, linking this with the growth of policing and prisons.[30] Those who claim that prosecutors' power is problematic argue that legislative change is a critical prerequisite to repairing a punitive apparatus that serves as a mechanism of social control over public safety and that criminalizes poverty.[31] Some point out, for example, that prosecutors are only in a position to charge a person for possessing a weapon as a convicted felon because the law criminalizes and punishes such conduct to begin with, while others emphasize the role of judicial discretion in sentencing decisions. Though the Sentencing Reform Act of 1984 aimed to reduce sentencing disparities by limiting judicial discretion, scholars have nonetheless argued that an effect of the sentencing guidelines and mandatory sentencing schemes more generally has been to augment prosecutors' control over defendants.[32] Since *United States v. Booker*, 543 U.S. 220 (2005) made the sentencing guidelines advisory, judges tend to depart downward from sentence recommendations, but the discretion they retain to give above-guideline sentences is also believed to increase prosecutors' leverage during plea agreement discussions.[33]

Scholarship on prosecutorial discretion at both the federal and the state level often focuses on prosecutors' power to induce defendants to plead guilty (rather than proceed to trial) and to recommend the sentences a defendant will face.[34] In the misdemeanor context, hasty and unscrupulous prosecutions can coerce innocent people to plead guilty. And these are innocent people who are disproportionately poor and Black, thanks to persistent class and racial disparities in the legal system. Prosecutors and defense attorneys who work on misdemeanors in particular are often overwhelmed by their caseloads, and more generally, as Alexandra Natapoff points out, "much of the misdemeanor process takes place on the fly, in bulk, without public scrutiny or even a public record."[35] Qualitative researchers have also noted the extent to which the adjudication of the guilt or innocence of those accused can appear to be more like an exercise in idiosyncratic courtroom politics than a fair process.[36]

Inconsistent and preferential charging decisions on the part of prosecutors have been another subject of scrutiny by social scientists. Focusing on assistant district attorneys, a study conducted in Los Angeles County and Indianapolis in 2003, for instance, sheds light on the ways that stereotypical conceptions of female credibility and victimhood can impact sexual assault prosecutions.[37] The study showed that state prosecutors are more likely to bring charges when victims have sustained injuries, suggesting that such physical indices of harm make a woman's claims of nonconsensual intercourse more credible.[38] A 1996 study based in Detroit similarly found that prosecutors were more likely to bring charges when victims' behavior conformed to gendered stereotypes of female victimhood—such as making a prompt report of the alleged rape, being sober at the time, and not voluntarily accompanying the defendant to his home.[39] Failing to possess any one of these characteristics, in some prosecutors' view, might compromise a victim's character and credibility, as they were believed to reflect poor judgment despite their irrelevance to the circumstances of a rape.

In the course of investigating inconsistencies in prosecutors' charging and declination decisions and critiquing the lack of transparency that characterizes these decisions, scholars have also drawn attention to instances of prosecutorial misconduct that have come to light.[40] These cases are often high-profile—in certain instances because of the powerful defendants involved. On several occasions, for example, the prosecutors I observed talked about the federal prosecution of former Alaska senator Ted Stevens. Stevens was charged in 2008 with failing to properly report gifts and was later found guilty.[41] After a whistleblower within the FBI alleged that the law enforcement agency and the US attorney's office had conspired to conceal critical evidence that might have acquitted Stevens, Judge Sullivan vacated the conviction and held the prosecutors in contempt. Though years had passed since the Stevens prosecutors' misconduct had been in the national news, a judge who presided over a case during my research still referenced Judge Sullivan's admonition to the trial team as a note of caution about the seriousness of a *Brady* violation.[42]

Declining Jury Trials

The potential for prosecutors to abuse discretion is especially concerning at a time when trials by jury in civil and criminal cases—and in state and federal courts—are the exception rather than the rule. In the criminal context, jury trials are rare and statistically in decline. Likewise, in the state context, the most recent available data from a sampling of the seventy-five largest counties in the United States show that in 2009, only 2 percent of defendants with felony convictions were tried by juries.[43] According to a different study, only 1,730 defendants were convicted by juries in 2014, while 76,163 pleaded guilty.[44] And a survey of state criminal and civil dispositions in fifteen and sixteen jurisdictions, respectively, yielded a similar result: only 1.1 percent of criminal cases were resolved by jury trial in 2009.[45] In federal court this figure is similar, with juries rendering verdicts in 1.52 percent of cases in 2020.[46]

In place of jury trials, about 97 percent of federal criminal defendants face conviction by guilty plea.[47] As a practical matter, some have argued that plea bargaining is necessary due to courts' limited resources and significant caseloads, since it offers an expedient alternative to trial.[48] Others have noted that inconsistent sentences recommended by prosecutors and imposed by judges lead to the disparate and discriminatory punishment of similarly situated defendants.[49] Guilty pleas have the added limitation of permitting little public insight into the considerations that inform particular negotiations or the *process* of negotiation between prosecutors and defendants.[50] Critics of plea bargaining highlight the risk that defense attorneys and judges will have little recourse if disputes arise as to fairness, quality of representation, or coercion of prosecutors.[51] Legal anthropologists have examined the secrecy of criminal procedures in non-US contexts as well. Leticia Barrera, for instance, has found that there are significant consequences of prosecutors' work being perceived as "secret and concealed from outsiders' view" in the Argentinean legal system.[52] Public hearings, Barrera explains, allow legal actors to curate a public image of themselves as accountable.

Proponents of plea agreements, however, have analogized them to the bargaining process that precedes civil settlement negotiations, which similarly take place in the shadow of a potential trial.[53] According to this logic, through plea agreements prosecutors are able to secure some punishment while conserving resources, and defendants are able to reduce their sentences. Critics of this bargaining model highlight obstacles to the creation of efficient and voluntary agreements, noting, for example, that prosecutors' superior knowledge about the strength of their cases results in an asymmetrical relationship that pressures defendants to waive their right to a jury trial even when it is not in their interest to do so.[54]

Compared with colleagues who prosecute misdemeanors in state court, federal court practitioners are members of a relatively privileged group that has the time and resources to devote to screening, reviewing, and discussing the cases they have the discretion to prosecute or decline.[55] If the misdemeanor system attracts attention for the callousness and indifference it shows to its poorest and most vulnerable subjects, the federal system often comes into public view through the high-profile prosecutions of powerful defendants.

Although felony prosecutions in federal court receive more scholarly attention than the misdemeanor process, there is a notable dearth of empirical data concerning the deliberations and decision-making practices of federal prosecutors' routine work. Prosecutors' off-record and unselfconscious behavior can offer insight into how they ascribe personal and social meaning to their work generally, beyond individual cases.

The mysterious character of prosecutorial discretion has made it ripe for legal and interdisciplinary theorizing. One topic of interest is the extent to which legal, practical, and normative constraints affect prosecutors' charging and declination decisions. Austin Sarat and Conor Clarke, for example, have noted that prosecutors are guided both by an instrumental calculation as to whether a prosecution is likely to result in conviction ("*Can* I prosecute successfully?") and by a concern with matters of culpability, equity, office policy, and resource conservation ("*Should* I try to prosecute successfully?").[56] It is this second formulation of discretion, which lies between the sovereign power Carl Schmitt conceived in his examination of what constitutes exceptions to the reach of law and the more banal framing of discretion as a "gap in the ordinary process of administration," that Sarat and Clarke suggest warrants further exploration.[57]

Sarat and Clarke's formulation of prosecutorial discretion as something more than the absence of rigid legal constraints can be taken further. The ethnographic research that is the basis of the chapters that follow demonstrates that federal prosecutors' conversations about particular cases and defendants were also conversations about the reach and limits of federal law. But what made these conversations concrete were their references to the sovereign power exercised by *jurors*, who would be at liberty, through their ability to render not-guilty verdicts despite evidence to the contrary, to define the law's exceptions. Prosecutors made sense of their discretion, in other words, by imagining the discretion that would be exercised by the laypeople who might serve as their jurors. It was this interplay—between the decision-making authority and practices of lay and professional legal actors—that prosecutors invoked conversationally to make decisions they believed were ethically defensible in the absence of legal clarity.

This was particularly true of cases in which prosecutors self-consciously acted in ways they believed showed mercy to defendants. One prosecutor, for example, described a case in which a pregnant mother of a young child accepted thousands of dollars to deliver a package of drugs to someone in an American airport. She knew she was being asked to commit a crime but insisted she had no choice—she needed the money to settle debts from a medical procedure for one of her family members. Though the AUSA assigned to the case could have charged the woman with violating the law, he refused to do so—he told me that if he had, he would not have been able to "sleep at night." In framing his decision to decline the case, however, juror discretion was central to his thinking. No juror, he contended, would convict a person in the defendant's position if it would mean spending taxpayer money to incarcerate her for several years in the United States. If he *did* prosecute the case, he thought aloud, he would count the defendant's information regarding the trafficking scheme as cooperative to the point of warranting significant leniency, hope for a sympathetic judge, and refrain from "fighting the defense" on motions for a downward sentence departure. From the moment the prosecutor received a call about a case like this one, he said, jurors were in the back of his mind: "I'm standing up in court in my head and pitching it to a jury and asking, 'Do they give a shit?'"

The impact of this kind of mercy in the criminal legal system is, however, viewed as questionable by other legal scholars.[58] Dan Markel, for example, notes that "the good intentions underlying calls for compassion through mercy provide no real justification for these efforts. . . . [F]rom the perspective of equal liberty under law, grants of mercy based on compassion are as problematic as grants of mercy based on caprice, sovereign grace, corruption, or bias."[59] Markel's point about uneven and idiosyncratic applications of mercy raises significant questions about the implications of prosecutors' reliance on fictional jurors' sympathy as grounds for declinations. Refraining from prosecuting a case to show mercy to an accused person, for example, has been demonstrated to systematically fail to redress wrongs in particular types of cases, including prosecutions of rape.[60]

Research that illuminates how prosecutors understand themselves to exercise discretion does not address the normative question of whether references to invented jurors exacerbate injustices endemic to a legal system plagued by socioeconomic and racial inequity. What it does, instead, is offer a glimpse into how prosecutors manage the inherent contingency of their work—an enterprise in which laypeople are perceived to play a central role. The fact that the AUSAs I observed perceived their own discretion to be limited by that of lay decision makers suggests that prosecutors felt ethically constrained, at least in part, when making discretionary decisions.[61] By prosecutors' accounts, jurors introduced extralegal and commonsense understandings of fairness into their decision-making process that informed, and in some cases guided, case decisions such as those discussed in the next chapter. At the same time, the outward-looking and self-referential practice of invoking hypothetical and disembodied jurors—which tethered prosecutorial discretion to juror discretion in the prosecutors I observed—brought social knowledge into the process of interpreting and enforcing the law. Though real jurors did not participate in such discussions or in the broader work of federal prosecution, the AUSAs I studied approached nearly every aspect of their jobs with consideration of laypeople—that is, laypeople of their own invention.

2

Imagining the Jury

We can never survey our own sentiments and motives, we can never form any judgment concerning them, unless we remove ourselves, as it were, from our own natural station, and endeavor to view them as at a certain distance from us. But we can do this in no other way than by endeavoring to view them through the eyes of other people, or as other people are likely to view them. . . . We endeavor to imagine our own conduct as we imagine any other fair and impartial spectator would examine it.

—Adam Smith, *The Theory of Moral Sentiments*

I did not arrive at the US attorney's office expecting to hear much about jurors. Though it stood to reason that prosecutors would be consumed with anxiety during jury selection proceedings, trials were few and far between for most line attorneys. And most of the prosecutors I spoke with acknowledged that they had almost no expectation that the cases they worked on would be decided by juries.

Yet in the course of dozens of conversations with attorneys from every unit in the office—including those with both criminal and civil dockets—jurors emerged as a central and shared preoccupation. "They are in the back of my mind when I don't even have the case," one AUSA explained to me. From the moment a federal case was brought to his attention over the phone—often by an FBI agent eager to confirm that an investigation yielded enough evidence to start making arrests—he said that he imagined himself "standing up in court in my head and pitching it to a jury." And he drafted indictments with fictional jurors in mind because, as another prosecutor explained, "There's always an audience."

Numerous AUSAs in the office's civil and criminal divisions agreed that it was important to think about juries early in a case owing to the possibility that the weakest target of an investigation would exercise his or her right to a jury trial. One prosecutor recalled losing a case because a "small fish" in a group of many targets chose not to plead guilty. In other instances, prosecutors were assigned cases long after the defendants had been indicted. In one such case, the prosecutor expressed regret that he had not previously considered how to present the relevant evidence to jurors.

Hypothetical jurors are useful to federal prosecutors for several reasons. First, they help prosecutors to impose order on their otherwise complex work. Invoking an imagined jury and thinking aloud about how its members would interpret a piece of evidence or hear a particular argument allows one to build the case in a more straightforward way— everything is anchored by the question of what will be intelligible and persuasive to laypeople. Second, hypothetical jurors provide prosecutors with a shared basis for collaboration and productive disagreement. Telling your trial partner they are wrong, abrasive, or confusing is difficult—it is far easier to steer case preparation and strategy by invoking the perspective of an imagined juror who might find them, well, wrong, abrasive, and confusing. Third, hypothetical jurors prove useful for thinking about what is actually criminal in the case. Something might violate the letter of the law, but juries introduce a social dimension to evaluation that can, depending on context, recast a criminal act as trivial wrongdoing or even "everyday justice."[1] Finally, imagined jurors offer a limited ethical check on prosecutorial and investigative behavior. Because the case ultimately has to be made *for the jury*, it has to come together in a way that will not violate jurors' sense of fairness or goodness. No matter how bad a defendant might be, most jurors—prosecutors imagine—will not want to learn that evidence was collected against them was gained dubiously, deceptively, or even illegally. In sum, prosecutors spend much of their time thinking inside the box—that is, with hypothetical juries—because it makes the work of prosecution possible.

Jury Appeal as an Evaluative Lens

By prosecutors' accounts, criminal cases fell into two broad categories: those that were *reactive* and those that were *proactive*. Reactive cases were prepared after an alleged crime had taken place. One such case I learned about involved a woman who had been stopped at an international airport with stacks of hundred-dollar bills in her luggage and a fake passport in her purse. An on-duty prosecutor received a phone call from an Immigration and Customs Enforcement agent who had detained her. This prosecutor was tasked with evaluating the facts and recommending a course of action to his supervisor. The on-duty attorneys who evaluated these kinds of situations were expected to handle a potential case from intake through trial, so a future jury's likely reaction to them and to the evidence was highly relevant.

AUSAs prepared proactive cases, in contrast, as investigations were underway. These cases sometimes required that prosecutors actively collaborate with other law enforcement agents. For the duration of an investigation, they would occasionally advise agents about the weight, necessity, and admissibility of evidence, as well as their own ability to prove each element of the crimes they would charge. Prosecutors thus made numerous decisions about investigative techniques and the adequacy and strength of evidence in conjunction with employees of federal agencies including the FBI—decisions all attuned to what they believed a hypothetical jury would think.

With both reactive and proactive modes of case preparation, federal prosecutors framed their concerns about their cases in terms of jurors' likely opinions of them. As prosecutors decided whether to bring charges against a defendant, for example, there was frequent talk of the jury appeal of evidence and witnesses. In some prosecutors' formulations, assessing jury appeal was likened to asking, "If I were a juror, what would I think?" Sometimes this meant considering whether a jury might feel that a case should be prosecuted at all, even if, legally, it could be. Sometimes these considerations convinced prosecutors to dismiss a case. As one AUSA put it, a case with "zero jury appeal" could lead to hostility not just from juries but also from the judge—something that no prosecutor wished to invite.

Those who worked on cases involving allegations of bribery were particularly attuned to the difficulty of explaining why their prosecutions should matter to jurors. In one case from the office, for example, a public official accepted money from people he knew well. The AUSAs worried that jurors might interpret these transactions as little more than a bit of well-intentioned hospitality among friends. This kind of concern prompted another prosecutor to encourage agents to record conversations whenever possible—a recording could at least help to give some indication of what the parties involved intended by a seemingly criminal act. Further, it might allow a prosecutor to demonstrate that the person did in fact take money in exchange for carrying out official acts. Beyond bribery cases, prosecutors also worried at times about prosecuting drug dealers or gang members caught up via the aggregation of defendants under racketeering law. Would jurors sympathize with victims who themselves engaged in violent criminal activity? It was not always clear.

A number of AUSAs I studied shared that they understood their job to revolve around "making jurors care." The onus was on a prosecutor, they said, to explain why seemingly innocuous acts—such as many obscure white-collar crimes—are not only criminal but socially harmful. Prosecutors differed on whether it was always possible to do this successfully. Some were skeptical, while others held that any case could be made appealing to a juror if it was presented properly. Imagined jurors thus prompted reflection on how to articulate the societal implications of, as one AUSA put it, everything from "shoplifting bubble gum to committing murder—and everything in between."

One case type, in addition to bribery, that could prove challenging was the structuring case. People are charged with structuring for deliberately limiting the increments of money involved in bank transactions to avoid triggering a federal reporting requirement. Most AUSAs I talked to agreed that structuring—while very much against the law and relatively easy to prove—was almost completely devoid of jury appeal. Multiple prosecutors bemoaned the difficulty of explaining to jurors that a law can both sound like an arbitrary regulatory requirement *and* be worthy of enforcement. Still, when charging a defendant with structuring, some prosecutors tried to make their case more compelling either by linking the charge to another underlying crime, such as participation in a larger illegal financial scheme or a terrorist plot. Another prosecutor suggested jurors would still be reluctant to find someone guilty for something that could be an oversight, as they worried that their own failure to fill out all required paperwork for jury service could be considered a violation of the law. Other factors that contributed to prosecutors' perceptions of jury appeal, for both structuring and other charges, included the intelligibility of the evidence they would present to jurors and the sympathy jurors might feel for the defendants or victims of alleged crimes.

Negotiating the Credibility of Witnesses

Even if a case has jury appeal, my interlocutors shared, you will not get a guilty verdict if your witnesses are not viewed as credible. This was another common theme in my conversations with AUSAs, most of whom said that the likability of a witness was a critical factor in their usefulness for a case. In fact, some shared that they had even selected or substituted witnesses based on anticipated jury impressions. Negative impressions could stem from a witness's personality or from their profession or status—prosecutors were at times anxious about putting law enforcement agents or cooperating witnesses on the stand due to possible negative reactions from jurors. Still, if it were not possible to make the case without, say, a police officer or an abrasive, rude, or dishonest witness, prosecutors were left with the option of using direct examinations to elicit more positive impressions.

The greatest challenge here, discussed further in chapter 5, was presenting cooperating witnesses, who, based on their status as former associates of the defendant, made them always potentially suspect. Despite believing that cooperating witnesses would testify truthfully as a condition of their promised sentence reduction, prosecutors worried that jurors would view cooperators as criminals willing to say anything to help their own case. Prosecutors who had met and spoken with cooperating witnesses dozens of times were inclined to believe their testimony, but they acknowledged the difficulty of trusting someone whose previous criminal activity perhaps fostered a negative first impression. One AUSA tackled this problem by attempting to put herself in the position of a juror hearing such a witness for the first time without the benefit of pretrial contact. This imaginative exercise convinced her that jurors would be skeptical, particularly in light of the judge's explicit instruction that cooperating witnesses' desire for leniency could present a conflict of interest and should be weighed carefully in evaluating their credibility.

Stories of acquittals in cases with highly unappealing cooperators were shared anecdotally in the US attorney's office as warnings of the perils of disregarding jurors' possible perceptions. In one case, for example, a cooperator had used racist language in a text message, which the prosecutor believed to be harmful to their cause. Any attempt at justifying or minimizing such language, he explained, would create a "sideshow" if the case proceeded to trial and would make his support for this witness's credibility personally uncomfortable. Attention to jurors' perceptions of testimony as offensive prompted some AUSAs to ask cooperators to think carefully about the language they used during investigations. One prosecutor, for example, explicitly told a witness not to curse because—although this was not improper or illegal—it might be off-putting to future jurors.

Prosecutors also evaluated case agents' credibility with jurors in mind. One prosecutor noted that he routinely considered how grand jurors and potential trial jurors might react to the agents who sat across the table from him. This AUSA said that he tried to imagine what a "random person off the street" would think, and he incorporated this perspective into his own preparation and strategy. With law enforcement agents, however, prosecutors sometimes found themselves working with actors devoted to other metrics of professional success. Other agencies had different criteria for professional advancement, for example, and so the metric used to determine the quality of an investigation—such as number of arrests arrests—could, AUSAs pointed out, become their overriding concern. For prosecutors, this approach was backward. As one explained to me, he would never arrest a target unless he was certain he could win at trial. Because the professional recognition conferred on agents for making probable cause–based arrests encouraged them to keep investigations moving and could lead them to pay less attention to other evidentiary issues, some prosecutors saw it as part of their job to convince agents to remember that all of their work was part of building a case for a trial—and should be planned and executed accordingly.

In another illustrative account, a prosecutor recalled a meeting in which prosecutors and case agents discussed their differing opinions about a case involving the sale of counterfeit goods. While reviewing the same evidence, the two sides differed strongly on its quality—and clarity. The prosecutors were not unimpressed but noted the case's complexity, implying that a thoughtful and intricate framing would be necessary to sway a jury. By contrast, the case agents saw little need for finesse—to their mind, the case was a slam dunk.

A slam dunk, of course, for the jury. Talk of hypothetical jurors was here and in so many other conversations a central feature of prosecutors' case preparation. Using such jurors as a reference point, prosecutors not only assessed potential witnesses' character traits but also scrutinized the evidentiary orientations of colleagues who carried out investigations and made arrests. Points of personal disagreement and competing interpretations of the same evidence were thereby attributed not to institutional, professional, or personality differences but to detached and hypothetical lay critics—stand-ins for the real jurors who might eventually pass judgment on their work.

Sympathy for Defendants and Victims

Another common theme in prosecutors' reflections on jury selection and trial preparation was concern that defendants might elicit sympathy. One prosecutor recalled a case in which a defendant came across as sympathetic in the very same video recordings that would be played to jurors as evidence of her wrongdoing. While accepting under-the-table payments, for example, this defendant asked her accomplices intimate and empathetic questions about members of their families. Upon seeing these warm exchanges, the prosecutor assigned to the case imagined that future jurors would find her likable, not culpable.

Likewise, prosecutors imagined their hypothetical jurors to be, in general, forgiving of those who broke laws to keep electricity running in their businesses, employed people during a recession, or served as scapegoats for more insidious individuals who were not indicted. A defendant who fraudulently gave tax refunds to a poor family might look more like Robin Hood than a criminal—and could one trust that a jury would convict Robin Hood?

Or a fraudster who was barely scraping by? In one case, a defendant was charged with failing to report the death of his mother, whose civil service retirement benefits he continued to receive. The defendant worked in a low-paying government job and used the money to support himself and an unemployed relative. The prosecutor assigned to the case recalled that the defendant was elderly and lived in poverty despite having this additional income. The prosecutor considered whether charging the defendant—and ultimately getting a felony conviction—before his planned retirement might preclude him from receiving his own pension benefits. Further, the prosecutor realized that when they thought of "civil service retirement benefits," jurors might think the defendant had pocketed sizable sums of money. In reality, according to the prosecutor, it was "very little month-to-month." On the other hand, given the poor state of the economy, it was possible jurors would react negatively to the prosecution of someone struggling to make ends meet. Ultimately, the prosecutor opted to pursue the case, though deferred the prosecution until after the defendant's retirement, thus saving his pension.

Sometimes, the AUSAs proved hesitant to show even limited mercy. Another case, involving the accidental death of children, appeared to deeply vex an AUSA as she considered whether to prosecute. She decided to engage the office in what some called "jury testing," or surveying colleagues on their reactions to get a sense of how future jurors might react. Opinions differed: some felt the defendant had suffered enough; others asserted that the AUSA had a responsibility to prosecute on behalf of the victims who no longer had a voice. She also spoke to members of the defendant's family to learn more about his character. She concluded that he was generally viewed as sensitive and conscientious—a finding that led her to worry that a case against him would be deeply polarizing. In the end, she decided to prosecute and privately expressed great disappointment when the defendant—found guilty—was *not* sentenced to prison. It appeared that this prosecutor had personally believed all along that the defendant deserved a particular fate, engaging in "jury testing" and other conversations only because she worried that a jury would struggle with the decision to convict someone who already lived with such intense grief because of a mistake.

Imagined jurors were also deployed regularly in cases that featured defendants who might seem more sympathetic than the victims. The Internal Revenue Service (IRS) was frequently cited as a "victim" that jurors would struggle to care about. One prosecutor explained the challenge of combating negative juror attitudes toward the IRS, noting that he "bent over backwards" to present the agency in the fairest light he could manage. Another colleague who tried tax cases lamented the fact that jurors often failed to distinguish between the IRS and his own employer, the Department of Justice, and he worried jurors would dislike the agency they thought he worked for.

Prosecutors considered other emotional responses that defendants or charges might elicit, too. For instance, prosecutors expressed ambivalence about taking on child pornography cases, as they guaranteed an outraged jury pool—and thus the near-impossibility of actually empaneling a jury of people who could confirm they would be fair and impartial. One prosecutor recalled a story in which merely learning the allegations in such a case prompted violent, almost uncontrollable, indignation from a prospective juror. But if distaste for a defendant caused problems—at least logistical ones—for child pornography cases, it was welcomed by prosecutors in most other case types. In one white-collar case, for instance, a prosecutor relished the fact that the defendant— tall, imposing, and expensively-dressed—was, as she put it, "a dick." It would be great for her case, she thought, if he was simply himself in court: bringing the same off-putting affectations from his work into the trial, where they would bolster the government's framing of his behavior as greedy and callous. She had not considered that he might use the trial to perform fake repentance, though perhaps she should have: in another case she tried, a wealthy older defendant appeared in court with a walker, limping to the witness stand. Sometimes defendants took the opposite approach: in one public corruption case, a defendant showed up in court looking, as the prosecutors put it, like he stepped out a fashion magazine. He presented himself as having "pulled himself up from his bootstraps," which the trial team worried made him seem relatable and even appealing to their imagined jurors.

As these examples suggest, hypothetical jurors provided prosecutors with a framework for scrutinizing the jury appeal of their cases, which in turn could serve as a means of assessing the intelligibility of charges, the credibility of witnesses, and the worthiness of their defendants for prosecution. As a malleable construct, hypothetical jurors also aided prosecutors' management of ongoing investigations, their evaluations of the sufficiency of available evidence, and their approaches to plea agreement discussions.

Interventions of Hypothetical Jurors in Prosecutorial Technique

Evidence and Investigations

Grand jurors have no shortage of questions. Prosecutors used the questions to reflect on their cases and map likely points of confusion for a future trial jury. Though federal prosecutors are not constitutionally required to present exculpatory evidence to grand jurors, the office that was the subject of this study conformed to a stricter internal policy mandated by the Department of Justice. If grand jurors asked hundreds of questions, a prosecutor told me, she would take that as a warning that twelve future trial jurors might do the same. Because grand jurors were often viewed as a guide for the way trial jurors might react, prosecutors sometimes asked grand jurors what they thought about particular pieces of evidence and how they could be framed more persuasively. Grand juror presentations also helped prosecutors gauge how relevant their evidence would seem to jurors at trial. Prosecutors thus kept track of grand jurors' reactions, making note of what might need to be addressed in subsequent questioning of witnesses.

Certain prosecutors I talked with felt they had no choice but to prosecute cases for which evidence would be lacking, which worried them because they believed these cases would be unappealing to the jurors they imagined. National security cases fell into this category, as agents could not always legally divulge the investigative techniques they deployed to lay decision makers due to statutory constraints. Some prosecutors considered jurors' incomplete access to—or lack of awareness of—classified information and evidence-gathering methods when deciding whether a case should be prosecuted. One prosecutor emphasized the importance of analyzing cases with reference to the partial evidence jurors would see rather than the full range of evidence known to those privy to investigations. Taking into account the evidence that jurors would have access to might mean prosecuting a suspected gang member with a lesser offense like tax evasion.

Most prosecutors I spoke with told me they regularly considered jurors' impressions of evidence as investigations were underway, as they believed this prompted greater reflection. One prosecutor noted that jurors served as a check on his personal decision-making process, spurring him to review his evidence "at every stage" to make sure he had enough and to consider its impact on jurors. According to this AUSA, case preparation was tethered to a future hypothetical trial in which jurors were the arbiters of even the most preliminary assessments of evidence. Based on their conclusions about how jurors might regard such evidence, prosecutors then developed organizational strategies for their investigations. These strategies ranged from how to select witnesses—including how to decide which individuals might testify on the government's behalf—to how to prepare them, such as in cases where prosecutors attempted to "flip" witnesses to have the cooperate against the target of an investigation.

As a general rule, informed by the intuitions they imputed to lay decision makers, prosecutors were reluctant to ask individuals with large roles in criminal schemes to testify against those in lower-level roles. In a fraud case, for example, a prosecutor lamented the fact that a low-level employee had been charged. Echoing this sentiment, other colleagues worried that future jurors would see company leaders turning on subordinates as something like family members testifying against one another and would react in ways that did not help the government's case.

Prosecutors' views on how the targets of their investigations should be monitored were also reflected how they thought future jurors might react to overzealous surveillance. One prosecutor described his horror upon learning that a law enforcement agent had been following a suspect using *an airplane*. He put an end to the investigation, citing jurors' likely intuitions that this approach to keeping track of a target was out of sync with reasonable law enforcement practices. He concluded that a future juror would, as he had done, wonder whether an agent who stalked a suspect from the sky was out of his mind.

Other prosecutors' ideas about how targets should be apprehended reflected their understanding of ethical norms they believed future jurors would share. One prosecutor described a white-collar case targeting a business owner who was suspected of being involved in a fraud scheme. After learning that another law enforcement agent planned to arrest this individual at work, the prosecutor proposed an alternative that he believed would be more palatable to future jurors. He was imagining a jury—that would not be convened for a while, if the case went to trial at all—hearing a defendant argue that he was an innocent man whose career was destroyed when he had been arrested and thus humiliated in front of his coworkers. This prosecutor further recognized *he*—not the law enforcement agents—would have to defend the decision to make the arrest in this way, which he wished to avoid.

The possibility that particular investigative approaches would violate lay citizens' ideas about fair evidence-gathering practices also loomed large for prosecutors. Here, again, concerns about how a jury might decide a case effectively amended the substance or prevented the enforcement of federal laws, particularly in the context of drug crimes. In one type of undercover narcotics investigation, agents offered to sell drugs to suspected drug dealers. Prosecutors worried that agents' deployment of this tactic, known as a "reverse," in which undercover agents posed as drug dealers and arrested drug-purchasing targets, would be perceived by jurors as unfair. But they nonetheless decided that jurors would see the criminality of the targets' conduct as outweighing the distasteful circumstances of such arrests when agents offered to sell drugs for large sums of money.

Another investigative technique that vexed some of the prosecutors is called the "home invasion reversal." Here, an undercover agent would alert targets to an opportunity to rob a local drug dealer's stash, which in reality was a location controlled by the agent. The agents would set a time and place for the robbery. Recognizing that hypothetical jurors might perceive this technique as deceptive or inducing otherwise law-abiding people to commit crimes, the prosecutors who weighed in on these investigations asked the agents they worked with to give targets several opportunities to change their minds and walk away, on video, before arresting them. In some cases, investigations were abandoned altogether. In one case, a prosecutor recommended an investigation be called off because the target that agents approached to carry out a robbery arrived on a bicycle and appeared harmless. The prosecutor imagined that future jurors could have concerns about entrapment or government overreach. Prosecutors were not so hesitant when targets arrived to the agreed rendezvous with their own weapons, bulletproof vests, and plastic wrist ties to immobilize victims. It was not hard to imagine jurors who would see these defendants as dangerous, violent, and thus worthy of the very aggressive tactics used to ensnare them.

Approaches to Plea Agreement Discussions

Pursuing plea agreements induced anxiety in many prosecutors, and so they contended that it was best to negotiate plea deals from the position of being prepared to try a case. Plea agreement discussions typically revolved around the strength of evidence, the seriousness of the charges, and the character of defendants. A federal prosecutor who tried drug and violent crime cases for which there was wiretap or video evidence, for example, routinely explained to defendants that he had never—in more than a decade of doing this work—seen a jury acquit a defendant in federal court. He indicated that the existence of such evidence meant jurors would readily understand what was at stake in the case, and so they would have no trouble coming to a verdict. Appealing to the accessibility and clarity of the evidence to future jurors, he then invited defendants to elicit their attorneys' perspectives on how jurors would likely view the case—a practice that encouraged defendants to appeal to differently imagined jurors.

Another prosecutor who tried gang cases made similar appeals during plea agreement discussions. He recalled telling a defendant that jurors' disdain would be immediate given that he had victimized children. This prosecutor shared that he imagined his future jurors not as individuals but as a generalized collective, picturing an "abstract model jury" in his head, all intently listening to everything he had to say—and more than willing to convict someone who hurt kids.

In a tax fraud case, another prosecutor encouraged a defendant to consider how a jury would view her conduct if the case went to trial. In this AUSA's view, a future jury would have "no patience" for a person who sought to enhance her material well-being by stealing federal tax dollars. The defendant's ultimate decision to accept a plea offer, in his view, was prompted by her acceptance of his narrative about how fictive lay decision makers would view the case. In a sense, she accepted the prosecutor's hypothetical jurors as all too realistic.

Notably, the plea deals proposed by the prosecutors I observed did not improve between the initial "show-and-tell" meetings and the approach of an actual trial—this was office protocol. But if prosecutors came into possession of information about defendants that they believed would make the defendant seem more sympathetic—or less culpable—to jurors, they might decide to make a better offer. During an interview, one prosecutor indicated that these decisions regarding the judgment of imagined jurors were "defendant-specific."

In other cases, locally and regionally specific attitudes of anticipated lay decision makers informed prosecutors' approaches to plea agreement discussions. A notable example of this was a case that involved the alleged abuse of a child. The lead prosecutor assigned to the case took seriously the fact that prospective jurors from this area would be likely to view the defendant's use of physical discipline as problematic. Had the case been tried in another part of the country, he explained, the group of prospective jurors might have included those with different approaches to punishing children. Because he believed that the jurors summoned to court would characterize excessive physical discipline as abusive, he felt confident he would be successful in securing a plea agreement.

Effects of Prosecutors' Consideration of Hypothetical Jurors

Although the chances of particular cases proceeding to trial were low, federal prosecutors relied regularly and heavily on hypothetical jurors in their work. My fieldwork suggests that this imaginative exercise had three purposes: it provided valuable preparation for a possible though unlikely jury trial; contributed to managing collaborative work and office relationships; and functioned as an ethical resource, helping them determine what might be "right" and "wrong" from the perspective of the public.

A first and obvious explanation of imagined jurors' salience in case preparation is lawyers' instrumental interest in anticipating how jurors might act in an actual trial. One prosecutor mentioned that despite having learned at a trial advocacy program that only 4 percent of cases ended with jury trials, she always wanted to be prepared. Anticipating the possibility that a case would be tried in court was analogized by some to preparing for an emergency. Prosecutors sought to make sure that from the moment a defendant was indicted the case could weather the contingencies attendant to trial. As one prosecutor explained, a case involving a cooperating witness could be turned on its head at a moment's notice if that witness was unexpectedly arrested on the eve of trial.

Empirical studies of lawyers' attitudes toward jurors have tended to focus on the strategic dimensions of attorneys' thought processes.

Rather than focus only on legal outcomes, however, anthropologists of law are increasingly attentive to aspects of legal practice that transcend instrumental considerations.[2] In the context examined here, it is clear that prosecutors' inordinate attention to jurors is not entirely attributable to ends-focused concerns such as (in the criminal context) obtaining convictions. As we have seen, prosecutors integrated talk of jurors into routine discussions—with one another and with me—as they assessed and debated particular decisions.[3]

Hypothetical jurors also served to facilitate more egalitarian and collaborative discussions with trial partners, supervisors, and colleagues from other federal law enforcement agencies. Rather than explicitly critique colleagues' opinions, lawyers frequently invoked the perspectives of hypothetical jurors. Divisive suggestions, in other words, were imputed to future lay decision makers. Imagined juror reactions thus served as legal fictions that allowed prosecutors to diplomatically reframe peers' approaches to cases in light of the different ways they might be interpreted by outsiders.

An office's particular organizational structure—including the way it is divided up and how many levels of oversight there are—also influences the opportunity for and quality of interactions between line attorneys and their supervisors. In the office that is the focus of this study, prosecutors often raised concerns about future jurors' views during preliminary meetings and conversations with law enforcement agents. These discussions, as I have noted, focused on the intelligibility of evidence and perceived credibility and character of witnesses, defendants, and victims. This practice was facilitated by the office's vertical structure, since prosecutors understood they would be responsible for each adjudicative phase of their cases through guilty plea or trial.[4]

In these contexts, AUSAs imputed opposing views to imagined lay onlookers. This technique allowed conflicting views to be presented in impersonal terms while keeping lay intuitions about justice at the center of case discussions. The diversely-constituted and unpredictable interpretations of future jurors thus raised the stakes of disregarding colleagues' divergent views. In an office subject to continual personnel rearrangement owing to the presidential appointment of new US attorneys, such a technique of neutralizing hierarchical distinctions was valuable.[5]

Though they offered a resource for prosecutors in conversation, concerns articulated in the name of hypothetical jurors did not necessarily win the day. In some cases, prosecutors' assessments of the jury appeal of their cases failed to change supervisors' minds. One prosecutor, for example, recalled being approached by an agent with a fraudulent billing case involving a physician and a family member. The prosecutor's inclination at the time was to look for evidence that larger amounts of money had moved in and out of the clinic. But supervisors wanted to proceed with the case immediately. After the defendants were sentenced to probation, the judge criticized the case, noting that neither defendant had a criminal record. The AUSA felt vindicated because the judge's instincts about the case mirrored those she had imputed to potential jurors. The prosecutor said this experience taught her to insist in subsequent cases that supervisors take her commonsense and jury-oriented critiques of cases more seriously.

Imagined jurors also contributed to prosecutors' interrogation of conceptions of justice.[6] In *Berger v. United States*, Justice George Sutherland famously described the prosecutor's role as seeing that "justice shall be done."[7] Though legal scholars and practitioners have since puzzled over the meaning of justice, the prosecutors I observed continually offered formulations of what they believed it entailed in particular cases. In so doing, they relied on hypothetical jurors' perspectives as a proxy for commonsense views that might not otherwise find explicit expression in their work.

Imagined jurors were useful in this exercise for several reasons. First, multiple and shifting identities and opinions could be imputed to them. That is, the varied and unpredictable responses of the laypeople prosecutors imagined authorized them to bring diversely constituted lay expertise into their case preparation. Second, hypothetical jurors' embodiment of distinct personas and perspectives, and their broad evaluative potential, gave them moral malleability for attorneys who invoked them. Depending on the particular perspective a prosecutor sought to advance, different juror characteristics and intuitions could be selectively emphasized.

Hypothetical jurors also offered prosecutors a resource with which to consider disparate meanings of justice in the context of different cases. Though the prosecutors who are the subjects of this study viewed their

central professional obligation as seeking justice, they articulated subjective intuitions about the fairness of decisions that varied from one
case and conversation to the next. Invocations of hypothetical jurors'
perspectives—and formulations of jury appeal in particular—often
brought the subject of justice into case assessments explicitly.[8] One prosecutor noted, for example, that inquiries into jury appeal were aimed at
determining whether cases were "fundamentally fair." In this prosecutor's view, jurors would differentiate between behavior that warranted
prosecution and behavior that did not.

Another prosecutor noted that the unpredictability of jurors' decision-
making processes mirrored that of his colleagues. He pointed out that
despite the fact that AUSAs shared professional training as lawyers and
carried out similar work, it was entirely possible to get twelve different
opinions from peers on how to approach case preparation or characterize evidence in opening statements. Another colleague explained that
everyone saw cases differently and that many wrangled internally with
doubt about what jurors would make of their judgment calls. Anticipating jurors' reactions to evidence and witnesses, however, was an inherently speculative endeavor. The variability of jurors' interpretations thus
prompted prosecutors to take a reflexive and flexible approach to evaluating particular pieces of evidence in their cases.

One case illustrates hypothetical jurors' relevance as prosecutors negotiated their professional roles and competing visions of justice. Here, a
prosecutor critiqued a defendant for taking bribes in dive bars and coffee
shops, where much of the surveillance evidence against him had been
gathered. A skeptical colleague intervened, highlighting the potential
negative reaction if he criticized the place where the defendant took the
bribes. If white-collar defendants routinely planned criminal activity on
golf courses without complaint, he argued, how would it look to criticize
a different defendant's use of more modest and widely accessible locales?
This colleague's decision to frame his intervention in this meeting from
a collective vantage point reflected an effort to present his views as en-
compassing those of listeners beyond his colleagues. In this instance, the
characterization of a case was revised with an eye toward incorporating
the concerns and intuitions of imagined others. Though jurors were not
privy to the interactions that purported to consider their perspectives,
they nonetheless had an outsized influence on prosecutors' work.

As these examples demonstrate, references to hypothetical jurors were often perceived to enhance the procedural justice of prosecutors' collaborative work, and their invocation helped ensure that each argument and counterargument was aired and considered on equal terms.[9] This is not, of course, to suggest that jurors functioned as an effective ethical constraint or that they necessarily facilitated just outcomes. To be sure, the idiosyncrasies of lawyers' views, even projected onto jurors, could vary as widely as those of empaneled deliberating jurors.

That hypothetical jurors play such an important role in prosecutors' work raises the question of the role of real jurors in our legal system, discussed in this book's conclusion. Sociolegal scholars who draw attention to the declining number of trials in the United States often assert the value of lay participation in symbolic terms. A return to a reliance on juries, they argue, might bring greater legitimacy and accountability to the legal system because juries serve as an external check on professional lawyers.[10] Ethnographic research in prosecutors' offices is uniquely positioned to draw out the basis and implications of this claim. It suggests that the role and practical workings of the jury system extend beyond the trial itself, with far-reaching effects on legal actors' expressions and reformulations of their ethical commitments. These findings demonstrate that the power of the jury system stems, in part, from its multifaceted influence on the lawyers tasked with enforcing the law fairly.

3

Storied Justice

I am not only accountable, I am one who can always ask others for an account, who can put others to the question. I am
part of their story, as they are part of mine. The narrative of
any one life is part of an interlocking set of narratives.
—Alasdair MacIntyre, *After Virtue*

The opening and closing statements AUSAs prepared for their cases were
usually concise, polished, and recited from memory. The process of creating such narratives, however, was far from neat. They were often written
in fits and starts: drafts were emailed, printed, returned with suggested
changes, revised, recirculated, and critiqued aloud during meetings with
colleagues. This was true, for example, of an opening statement that one
prosecutor prepared for a mortgage fraud case. Hunched over a pile of
notes in a windowless conference room, he glanced up from scattered
pages on the table in front of him. His audience of prosecutors, meanwhile, looked past him at an aerial image of a destroyed building that was
projected on a retractable screen. They set cell phone timers and peeled
their legal notepads to fresh pages. The story began:

> It was two o'clock in the afternoon when [the building] exploded. It was a
> gas explosion. The building was leveled by a powerful, violent blast. One
> woman died and five others were critically injured. It shook the entire
> block. Homes all the way down the street had their windows blown out,
> and [the building] no longer existed. The defendant knew about the explo-
> sion and that his property no longer existed. It was all over the local news
> all day. But the evidence will show that the defendant stood to gain hun-
> dreds of thousands of dollars by pretending the building was still there.

The defendant, the theory went, saw the explosion as an opportunity. Posing as a loan officer, he could pocket money for the building's

fictitious sale. He did this by submitting fraudulent mortgage loan applications to banks on behalf of straw buyers. For each loan obtained through this scheme, the defendant took a commission for himself.

Beginning the opening with a pile of rubble and casualties was a novel narrative flourish. Though the image appeared on the screen only briefly, it remained on the minds of the prosecutor's colleagues as they responded with suggestions. One said, "It's confusing. When you're sitting there, you think it's a case about arson, or national security, or weapons of mass destruction." A second noted, "It's a powerful picture. It has shock value. . . . It's a question of when you want to deploy it." And a third wanted to "go back to the vignette," asking how it could be made more succinct.

These reactions highlight several issues that are central to this chapter. First, they illuminate the collaborative process by which lawyers negotiate and rewrite narratives about their cases. They also reveal prosecutors' attention to the perspectives of future listeners. This particular case, like most in the office, was resolved by a guilty plea and never reached a jury. Nevertheless, prosecutors oriented their preparation around perspectives that they imputed to hypothetical jurors.

This process of narrative negotiation and revision became only more complex as prosecutors integrated witnesses' responses into their preparation for cross-examinations, summations, and rebuttals. Though prosecutors tried to anticipate what they would hear from the stand, they could not predict the language witnesses would use, events they might forget, or their responses to defense counsel's questioning. This uncertainty was compounded by the many decisions made as trials unfolded—including whether to call cooperators as witnesses and how to cross-examine defendants if they chose to testify.

A central insight that emerged from my observation of the prosecutors in the US attorney's office is that the process of rehearsing, discussing, and revising opening and closing statements encouraged prosecutors to negotiate the meaning of their professional and ethical imperative to seek justice. In the process of imagining jurors' perspectives, prosecutors brought clarity to their ideas about just prosecutions and the professional values that supported them. This finding complements anthropologists' observation that the opening statements shared in court are products of co-narration through which disputed life events are "transformed and fused into a coherent, authoritative, public narrative."[1] It also complements the research of cultural and linguistic anthropologists who understand identity formation as an interactive and "contextually situated" process that emerges through real-time discourse.[2] As prosecutors discussed the stakes of proposed revisions, they explicitly and implicitly defined the limits of their discretion.

Jurors at the Center of Opening and Closing Statements

Prosecutors' discussions of case narratives centered on jurors' potential interpretations of evidence. Although conjuring jurors' impressions was an inherently speculative endeavor, prosecutors nonetheless developed precise beliefs about their future lay decision makers. In some cases, prosecutors explicitly identified "average" jurors as middle-class individuals who were employed and lived in the suburbs.[3] In other cases, prosecutors' understandings of jurors stemmed from knowledge of family members or friends who shared characteristics in common with them (e.g., occupations, counties of residence) and were thus regarded as proxy jurors, as discussed in chapter 2.

When it came time to prepare opening and closing statements, the distinction between prosecutors and the jurors they imagined was ambiguous at best, as lawyers became surrogate jurors for each other. For some, the aim of preparation meetings was to brainstorm and refine language that might resonate with laypeople. For others, presentation style was a narrative priority, as prosecutors likened themselves to teachers. In both cases, jurors' perspectives were invoked and imaginatively enacted by prosecutors as part of a practice of distancing themselves from cases so that they could offer critiques from a position of detachment.[4]

Several prosecutors emphasized the importance of using analogies in opening statements that jurors might relate to. This included a lawyer who kept a list of details about jurors in front of her during opening statements and throughout trials. "If I have carpenters or teachers on my jury," she explained,

> I will try to phrase arguments to connect personally with them. If I am
> talking about money laundering or a narcotics-trafficking organization
> utilizing a black market exchange, I might focus jury addresses on some-

thing like "the tools of the trade of a narcotics officer" or "just like a carpenter has a hammer, nails, pens . . ." to engage them individually or "just like a nurse has medicine . . ." You address jurors keeping in mind all the time what their individual lives are like.

While preparing for a trial two years later, the same prosecutor said that she could tell jurors were receptive to her metaphors when she saw their "eyes light up" as she connected with them as individuals. This prosecutor said she thought of the jurors assigned to the cases she tried as *her* jurors. Even if jurors did not find her rhetorical efforts persuasive, another prosecutor explained, they might at least pay attention. When another colleague learned that several members of a jury were parents, she made an effort to use analogies that involved children, likening the use of circumstantial evidence, for example, to concluding that a child had eaten cookies after noticing crumbs on his face, chocolate on his breath, and an empty, open cookie jar beside him in the kitchen.

In the spirit of keying language used in opening and closing statements to jurors' likely experiences outside the courtroom, another prosecutor considered presentation styles that future listeners might be receptive to. "If you have a teacher or an auto mechanic," he explained,

> it is going to affect your argument in different ways. If you have a teacher, you want to be the outstanding student with answers to every question. If you have an engineer you want to give facts, weights, and percentages. If it's a hockey player you might use more aggressive language. You want to know that so you can craft the message. You don't move the facts around, but you adjust the presentation.

Consideration of jurors' divergent backgrounds thus prompted creative discussion of how cases might appear to observers unfamiliar with the details. Recognizing that people rely on analogies to reconcile informational gaps in everyday life, prosecutors eagerly reframed evidence to make it align with knowledge systems likely to be familiar to jurors.[5]

Other prosecutors searched jurors' responses to voir dire questions for clues about how to characterize evidence that might strike a layperson as counterintuitive. To disabuse jurors of the notion that fingerprints and DNA evidence were essential components of criminal investigations, for example, a prosecutor revisited her notes on jurors' television habits. If many of them reported watching crime shows like *CSI*, she incorporated this fact into her opening statements. She explained that jurors would learn from experts that unlike in popular legal dramas, DNA rarely solved cases in real life. By commenting on jurors' exposure to fictionalized law enforcement work, she hoped to manage their expectations and anticipate questions that might arise during their deliberations. In the context of a child abuse case, a different prosecutor prepared for a closing statement by revisiting the responses of jurors who believed that children could love parents who abused them. In his view, invoking jurors' understandings of the complexity of abusive relationships might bolster his own commonsense argument that the defendants' intermittent expressions of warmth and affection did not mitigate their guilt.

Making Evidence Intelligible

Opening statements, whose length could range from ten minutes to several hours, were selective by necessity—they were more like previews than full stories. This was by design. These statements were intended to offer jurors a bare-bones understanding of the charges and evidence and to transform complex or unpredictable testimony into simple narratives. A benefit of this approach, as prosecutors saw it, was the possibility that concise narratives would be more compelling and memorable than overly detailed or long-winded ones. To refine their case stories, prosecutors critiqued each other's presentations from the vantage point of hypothetical lay decision makers, allowing suggestions for revision to be articulated in impersonal terms as prosecutors scrutinized evidence with fresh eyes.

Although the critiquing process relied on the dubious assumption that prosecutors' concerns could be substituted in conversation for those of future jurors, many prosecutors nevertheless viewed their task in crafting opening statements as one of making the facts of a case and elements of a crime intelligible to an imagined lay audience. As part of this effort, they encouraged each other to transform evidence into "sound bites of key information," "simple thoughts," or language that a juror "could reasonably digest." As one prosecutor explained, "The more you can define factual issues to the jury and define the facts of the case they're going to have to decide, the easier it will be for them and the easier it will be for you." Another prosecutor referred to his professional obligation to translate legal language for laypeople as a "burden of coherence." Viewing this as a narrative burden, he added that "to the extent there are gaps and there are holes in what we can explain or in what we can make comprehensible to the jury, that's to our detriment. Anything—if you're missing a shoe, to analogize it, that's to my detriment. . . . Anything that is out of kilter contributes to doubt." Others conceptualized the task of teaching jurors about their cases as part of their duty to "close logical loops," "connect the dots," "marry up" different aspects of a crime, and "lay out" for jurors *why* particular pieces of evidence were significant. Exemplifying this approach, a supervisor suggested that paragraphs of an opening statement in a bribery case be revised to sound like a primer for jurors. Here, again, the imagined perspectives of individuals who lacked professional training that might prepare them to tackle legalese helped prosecutors reassess evidence in their cases.

Prosecutors often tried to use "colloquial," "conversational," "down-to-earth," "plain," and "everyday" language to aid jurors' comprehension of cases by crafting stories in terms used and heard outside of court. A commitment to earning jurors' trust led a number of the prosecutors I observed to try to communicate in an informal and conversational manner and to avoid beginning with or relying on PowerPoint slides. The stakes of establishing a rapport with jurors, in the view of some prosecutors, were high. One prosecutor thought that if he seemed like someone a juror would want to "hang out" with, that person might be more likely to listen to and trust him. Other prosecutors were attuned to whether they (or their trial partners) had "some kind of simpatico" or felt a personal connection with a particular juror during voir dire.

One of the largest challenges, one prosecutor reflected, was composing a narrative the jury would believe.[6] Another emphasized the importance of using language that would "resonate" with her listeners, and others pointed out that jurors who believed in *them*, as officers of the court, would be more inclined to believe their arguments. During preparation meetings for fraud, drug, and gun cases, prosecutors distinguished between the level of precision and detail one might expect from an oral story like an opening statement as opposed to a written brief. In a brief, a prosecutor explained, it might be appropriate to list the monetary values of dozens of loans or note the number of days between transactions, but in the context of an oral opening statement, quantitative description did not contribute much to jurors' understanding. As he listened to a mooted opening statement, this prosecutor discouraged his colleague from offering a narrative in which documenting quantitative DNA data took precedence over providing a more colloquial account of the evidence. In this prosecutor's view, an opening suffered if it was "too wordy, too full of legalese, and too complex." In another case involving allegations of illegal gun possession, a prosecutor's opening statement was criticized in similar terms. "This sounds as if you wrote it as opposed to 'let me tell you what happened . . .' like you're just *talking* to the jury," another prosecutor noted. "If you were just telling them what happened, you'd use different words. It would sound different from the way it would if it was a scholarly lecture." In this prosecutor's view, an opening statement should sound like a story rather than a legal brief.

Some prosecutors who took this approach did so because they presumed that jurors who failed to understand evidence or got lost in its detail might mistake their confusion for defects in a case. This was true, for example, of prosecutors who tried RICO cases and worried that if jurors heard a story involving numerous defendants their confusion might lead to acquittals. This concern led one prosecutor to suggest that a colleague's presentation was too "nuanced and detailed" and not straightforward enough.

A case that involved the theft and shipment of cars prompted a similar response from a colleague who thought that

> the details in the beginning really jump out, but I think the opening is too detailed. This is a simple case. Name the steps. Step one: the car is stolen. Step two: you let the car cool off by leaving it off the street. Step three: you clean the car. Then you warehouse it and change the VIN number. After the warehouse you put the car in a crate. It's a process with five basic steps for how to steal a car.

Earlier in this prosecutor's group meeting, a different colleague had commented that the jury might be confused by the fact that Homeland Security officers had authorized the stolen car's shipment as part of their investigation. Other prosecutors agreed that this detail did not "make the cut" for the opening, and its deliverer was persuaded that it would raise more questions for jurors than it would answer, and "ultimately, you want the jury to understand." In certain cases, prosecutors would underscore how defendants had gone to extreme lengths to make it difficult to understand what they had done, which amounted to a sophisticated effort to conceal their wrongdoing. One prosecutor, for example, noted how a fraud case he had worked on took *him* hours to understand, a fact he took advantage of in his presentation: "I put up a slide that looks incredibly complicated and I say 'look at this. The *defendant* made this complicated so that he wouldn't be here today.' So I embrace the complexity."

In other cases, references to fictive jurors' perspectives prompted discussion of substantive legal issues. For example, after a prosecutor had finished a run-through of a ten-minute opening statement for a child pornography case, a colleague remarked on the fact that the prosecutor had "described child pornography as child sexual abuse," asking, "Isn't that just a subset of child pornography?" In the discussion that followed, prosecutors fluidly tacked back and forth between the need to refine legal characterizations of sexually explicit images for lay listeners and for each other. Requests for a "better road map," topic sentences, and colloquial definitions highlighted the imagined jury's role as an editorial resource in the process of interactively constructing legal knowledge through conversational storytelling.[7]

Articulating Conceptions of Justice While Forming a Story

Sociolegal scholars have shown that stories play a vital role in legal actors' efforts to make sense of their experiences, actions, professional identities, and normative commitments.[8] The narrative form, these scholars argue, is critical to making the world orderly and intelligible. In a similar fashion, the prosecutors I observed sought to bring clarity to both their cases and professional commitments through their collaborative construction of opening and closing statements. As prosecutors critiqued colleagues' case characterizations, they explicitly and implicitly isolated narrative approaches that embodied personal and professional character traits they viewed as essential to their work. Prosecutors' self-consciousness about their perceived reliability and fairness featured prominently in their discussions. As one prosecutor, who had tried forty-seven cases and won all of them, commented, "I know I'm good at what I do and know how to differentiate myself from my opponents by showing I'm trustworthy, believable, likable, and have good evidence."

The AUSAs all agreed that opening and closing statements played a role in building and maintaining jurors' trust, but they took different approaches to demonstrating their credibility and articulated distinct professional values. One prosecutor, for example, might focus on ensuring that opening statement narratives aligned with evidence jurors would see or hear during trial. Another might seek to emphasize her preparedness, another might stress educating jurors about the law, and yet another might foreground corroborating evidence.

During discussions of opening statements, in particular, prosecutors spent time scrutinizing the specificity and accuracy of their characterizations of evidence. Underlying this effort was an assumption that inconsistencies introduced at a later point in the trial would call a prosecutor's character—and therefore arguments—into question. The stories prosecutors fashioned for jurors were thus regarded as "commitments" or promises to them. Violations of this trust were referred to as problems of "overcommitting," "overselling," or "overpromising" in opening statements. The following dialogue illustrates the conversational approach prosecutors took in sharing and critiquing the narratives they expected witness testimony to later support. The defendants in the case were charged with using a firearm to steal a car:

PROSECUTOR 1: OK. So you don't know who was standing on what side of the car or who said "get the fuck out of the car"? Be slow and deliberate: "The victims saw a shotgun and heard the words 'get the fuck out of the car' and, ladies and gentlemen, this is the shotgun they saw." Have the victims seen the gun?

PROSECUTOR 2: They say . . . the defendant was wearing a long . . . a trench coat and that he held the gun in front of him upright—in the middle. The female says she doesn't really know guns but she says her husband does and that it's not a handgun. That it's long and black . . .

PROSECUTOR 1: OK. They say black?

PROSECUTOR 2: Yeah.

PROSECUTOR 1: OK.

PROSECUTOR 3: You don't want [defense counsel] holding the gun
up and saying "have you seen this before?" and the victim saying, "I
don't think so. I don't really know."
PROSECUTOR 1: Definitely prepare them for that.

Anticipating that jurors might not hear evidence clarifying who held
the gun, a supervisor suggested that the deliverer of the opening statement highlight the insignificance of the detail she could not commit to.
"The defendant is criminally responsible for using a gun in furtherance
of a carjacking," the supervisor said, rehearsing a proposed revision of
the narrative aloud. "The evidence will show that even if the defendant
didn't tell you that it was his companion who carried the gun, they are
both criminally responsible." A colleague added that a succinct way to
help the jury "pull all the evidence together" was to note that the defendant "acted consistently with someone who knew the gun was there."

Although prosecutors generally agreed that precise language was ben-
eficial, they disagreed about the value of vagueness. Prosecutors often
consciously deployed imprecise language to reflect limitations in evidence, to the consternation of colleagues quick to critique "wishy-washy"
language—exemplified by adverbs like "somewhat" to characterize illegal
conduct. In one case, a prosecutor critiqued another prosecutor's appeal
to "common sense" on the grounds that it signaled that the trial team's
evidence was insufficient, which would require jurors to make an excessive inferential leap to convict the defendant. Common sense, in this lawyer's view, was too indeterminate and subjective for lay decision makers.
In another case, a prosecutor criticized a colleague for telling jurors in
the opening statement that they might "hear things" during the trial that
were at odds with the opening. Though the trial team had adopted this
approach to anticipate contrary arguments from defense counsel, this
colleague warned them that such phrasing might lead jurors to believe
they would hear something harmful to the government's case. "It implies
this case is so nuanced that if you don't get *all* of the details, you can't
convict," he continued. "But that's not the case at all."

Although prosecutors worried about the risk of being contradicted at
a subsequent point in the trial, they also did not want to be perceived as
withholding evidence in their opening statements that did not support

their cases. Several of the prosecutors I observed advocated for sharing ambiguous or unfavorable information during opening statements, a practice known as "fronting" evidence. Using this technique, they hoped to demonstrate their candor to jurors—a quality that some prosecutors associated with their effectiveness as trial attorneys. In one case, a prosecutor was not certain how defense counsel would use evidence that a defendant only offered commissions on some of the bribes he solicited, and so a supervisor encouraged him to mention this detail in his opening, lest jurors conclude this was a deliberate omission on the part of the trial team.

Many prosecutors also felt that demonstrating their preparedness by memorizing details in their cases would signal to jurors that they took their jobs and audience seriously. In a gun possession case, for example, a prosecutor emphasized the narrative value of confidently describing the name, model, size, and place of origin of the weapon in question. "I've done a lot of gun cases," she explained. "I hold up the gun and say 'this is a BLANK,' without looking down, because that goes to *my* credibility. I *know* this gun. This is *my* case. You're going to have it in your hand and look right at them as you say it." Echoing this sentiment, another prosecutor agreed that references to minutiae "show you know what's going to happen—you're in command of this case. Like, 'I know all the facts and I'm going to tell you, some of these witnesses are going to be a little problematic, and here's why: The stuff they did was illegal.' So to me it just shows you have control of the case."

Detailed references, these prosecutors believed, might enhance their credibility by exhibiting their own factual proficiency. Correspondingly, considering the value conferred on precision, prosecutors' misstatements of evidence or displays of inconsistent facts via visual aids were sharply criticized by their colleagues because of their anticipated effect on jurors.

Prosecutors were also conscious that the language they used could affect perceptions of the criminality of defendants' conduct. Prosecutors thus tried to underscore the illegal dimensions of defendants' behavior. Comments from a meeting in preparation for a car theft trial exemplified this approach. Here, a prosecutor pointed out that "when you use words like 'contracts' and 'employees' it makes it seem like a legitimate business. You may want to do a little up front on the legitimate aspect of the business but say that we're talking about the illegitimate thing. This will give context. So throw it up front and introduce the concept." Another colleague offered advice along similar lines, suggesting the lead prosecutor "explain all the things she did in her *illegal* enterprise to *steal* cars." Rather than use words and phrases like "businesswoman," "business associate," "partner," and "profit for her business," he recommended language that drew attention to the defendant's wrongdoing—such as "coconspirator" and "illegal enterprise." This would have the effect, the logic went, of alerting jury members of their skepticism regarding the defendant's claims.

Another case raised similar concerns for a prosecutor who observed:

> I don't think I heard the word "kickback" once. It was like, "he made a recommendation and he got a share." That sounded pretty legitimate to me. I would say, instead of "he helped get them hired, he got a piece of the action," "he helped get them hired, he got a kickback." It's a kickback case and I don't think we say "kickback."

Another colleague who participated in this meeting suggested the opening statement be revised to make the case sound "bribe-ier." Because in this colleague's view the prosecutor making the opening statement had already mastered a strong delivery, not much more was needed to nail it—just "tightening it up and bribing it up a little more, frauding it up, and extorting it up a little." These comments echoed others that colleagues made in criminal cases, such as recommendations to use the term "the defendant" (rather than "he" or "she"), refer to cooperators as "coconspirators," and choose words like "hitting" in child abuse cases instead of "discipline" to stress the illegality of the conduct they were describing. Prosecutors also recommended characterizing defendants' actions in the active voice when possible: "he told her he hid the files," for example, rather than "he told her the files were locked up."

Prosecutors' narrative work was thus guided by what they felt was their obligation to precisely identify and explain the significance of the laws at issue in their cases to encourage jurors to view defendants—or their conduct—as criminal. Discussion of a convicted felon charged with carrying a firearm was instructive in this regard:

PROSECUTOR 1: You started the opening with the *law*—and I wouldn't. I always start with a grabber fact—and I'm not a big fan of starting with the law. You could say, "The defendant had just committed a traffic infraction" with just two or three sentences of description—just hitting them with a fact. Something brief. Like "they were on patrol in a high-crime area and saw someone speeding. But what happened next was quite unusual." . . .

PROSECUTOR 2: Is it? I wouldn't say it's quite unusual. . . .

PROSECUTOR 3: I disagree. . . .

PROSECUTOR 2: If you don't start with the law . . . People will be thinking, "Why is the US government caring? This is just a gun case." So the *federal* part is important—because why are we here on a gun case? Why is the government wasting its time and resources? . . .

PROSECUTOR 3: . . . It's illegal under *federal law* . . . .

PROSECUTOR 1: You've got to get into the cadence by looking at the jury and just grabbing them. . . . "What happened next was quite unusual. And why?"

PROSECUTOR 3: But a lot of people don't know carrying a gun is a crime. Usually I'd agree with you, but not here. It's a matter of style; there's no right way to do it. . . .

PROSECUTOR 1: See, I disagree. It just doesn't grab you. . . .

PROSECUTOR 4 [THE AUTHOR OF THE DRAFT STATEMENT]: I read four opening transcripts for gun possession cases and they *all* started with the law. . . .

Although all the prosecutors agreed the question of whether an opening should begin with a hook meant to grab and engage listeners or instead outline the law a defendant was charged with breaking was an important one, the stakes of this decision for some of the prosecutors who discussed it were higher. What if jurors saw nothing wrong with the defendant's conduct? The prosecutors who thought it was imperative that the law be mentioned straightaway emphasized that failing to do so might confuse jurors or, worse, make them question the prosecutors' judgment. Ideas about narrative sequence were thus tied to prosecutors' conceptions of their professional roles. Accepting the risk of boring jurors, the one prosecutor believed that the trial team's obligation to assert the legitimacy of a case should trump concern about how to animate the events in their story.

AUSAs also sought to demonstrate their credibility by presenting themselves as neutral purveyors of independent and mutually reinforcing evidence of wrongdoing. This let jurors do the work of putting together the story. This approach was also designed to emphasize that distinct pieces of evidence could separately lead a juror to the same conclusion about a defendant's guilt. Jurors could interpret complementary, overlapping, or "lined-up" accounts of a defendant's actions, in other words, as evidence of their facticity. In contrast to presentations that appeared to rely on discrete pieces of evidence (e.g., surveillance footage, DNA evidence, eyewitness testimony), as though each existed in a vacuum, the skillful closing statement or rebuttal served to direct jurors' attention to "all those things taken together."

The significance of corroborating evidence emerged with particular force during a child abuse prosecution. To support her theory of the defendants' medical neglect of the victims, the case's lead prosecutor planned to show the jury medical records that documented doctors' referrals to seek immediate follow-up treatment and the defendants' subsequent failure to follow through. She would then show the jury records generated by administrators listing numerous appointments the defendants had canceled or missed. During a conversation I had with this prosecutor during a commute home one day, she described this as "leaving no stone unturned," allowing the jury to "cross-check" her claims. This prosecutor, like others, pointed out that offering several accounts of the same conduct would reinforce her own credibility if jurors chose not to believe a particular witness.

Prosecutors also considered the possibility that jurors might view witnesses' later narratives as corroborating their opening statements. Recognizing the additive value of these contextualizing accounts, one prosecutor described them as "a stamp on all the arguments and evidence you've presented" and a means of "buttressing" particular witnesses' credibility. In reference to a cooperating witness's testimony, another prosecutor noted that "it bolsters my credibility when the jury says 'yeah, we heard about that before in the opening.'" By the same token, jurors might notice aspects of opening and closing statements that were inconsistent, and so colleagues would often urge trial partners to reconcile their own competing narratives before trial.

Don't Be an Overzealous Prosecutor

While discussing opening statements, prosecutors also critiqued behavior that a hypothetical juror might consider *overzealous*. Though they never defined this quality explicitly, prosecutors articulated different indices of it, such as appearing excessively argumentative, confrontational, disrespectful, or dismissive when characterizing witnesses or evidence. A juror's presence, even in hypothetical form, thus invited prosecutors to share their own commonsense understandings of how to distinguish reasonable from excessive advocacy in criminal prosecutions. Another exchange in the mortgage fraud case with which I began this chapter illustrates the shifting meaning of this unwanted attribute. In the following excerpt, one prosecutor challenged the trial team's decision to have the defendant's mother testify against him in court even though her name, address, and signature on forged loan applications implicated her in the scheme.

> PROSECUTOR 1: OK, so you could go through it like that. . . . You're getting the mother to testify?
> PROSECUTOR 2: Yeah, she's going to say that she never signed any documents . . .
> PROSECUTOR 3: Prep the jury for that, so they don't think we're being overzealous . . .
> PROSECUTOR 1: You're getting his sister, too?
> PROSECUTOR 2: Yeah, she's listed on the form as a loan processor.
> PROSECUTOR 3: At some point, you should allude to the unpleasant task the defendant has forced the government to do. . . .
> PROSECUTOR 1: Is there another way to do this? Could you get tax returns . . . for the mother?

Here, the one prosecutor made his concern about government overzealousness explicit. Despite the legality of calling a defendant's family member as a witness, he explained after the meeting that he found this tactic problematic: "I could understand this in a murder case, but this is fraud. How is the government going to appear? If I have a father, and he's not going to lie on the stand, what good is he? If I have a kid and I won't lie for him, what's the point?" His hesitation about bringing the defendant's mother and sister to court reflected his intuition that jurors might feel—as he did—that requiring family members to testify against each other was wrong somehow. At best, another prosecutor put it, the practice was "kind of distasteful." Prosecutors thus ascribed their commonsense idea about fair mortgage fraud prosecutions to the trial team's future audience of lay decision makers. The prosecutor who had initially asked whether the mother could testify found this argument compelling and came up with an alternative approach that helped his colleagues prove the fraudulence of the loan application with tax documents instead.

Prosecutors' sensitivity to jurors' perception of overzealousness was also part of discussions about how to characterize cooperating witnesses. Prosecutors did not want to endorse the behavior that brought cooperating witnesses into contact with law enforcement officers, so they navigated this fraught relationship carefully. In one conversation, for instance, a prosecutor critiqued her colleague's description of cooperating witnesses as "crooks" and "fraudsters," arguing that even though she had used that very kind of language in a different case of her own, in that context the cooperating witnesses weren't testifying, so she "had a little more license to dump on them. There's another way to say it—not as pejoratively." Cooperating witnesses presented a dilemma for prosecutors who sought to differentiate themselves from self-confessed criminals.

Unsurprisingly, opening statements that appeared to vouch for, praise, or depict cooperating witnesses as victims were criticized by AUSAs. One could not predict exactly what such witnesses would say or how truthful their testimony would seem to jurors. In one case, a prosecutor responded to a colleague's comment that a cooperator wanted to start his life again with a clean slate by commenting, "Unless you're really confident the jury's going to buy that he turned his life around, I wouldn't vouch for it. . . . You don't know how this guy is going to come across." In this context, the witness was charged with crimes he committed after signing an agreement with the government—a fact that this prosecutor believed would tarnish jurors' opinions of him and undermine their confidence in lawyers who appeared to take him at his word.

In another case, an AUSA encouraged a colleague to use the impersonal construction "the evidence is going to show" rather than "we're going to provide evidence" when characterizing a cooperating witness's testimony so as to insulate herself from responsibility for his statements and avoid creating the impression she vouched for the witness. Prosecutors typically worried that if jurors were asked to believe the testimony of a witness they disliked, they might hold the trial team accountable.

Prosecutors also critiqued opening statements that appeared to align the government too closely with certain kinds of witnesses. One opening statement, for instance, discussed witnesses who were undocumented immigrants. A supervisor objected to a section of a draft that described such witnesses as gathering money to pay bribes from their "hard-earned paychecks." He worried that some jurors might share then-president Donald Trump's stance on immigration and so view undocumented witnesses as earning money at the expense of law-abiding citizens. "I don't know how much we want to make them into victims," he said.

Others more explicitly associated the value of precise language with their roles as "honest brokers" who refrained from "overt argumentation." A prosecutor's critique of one of his colleague's opening statements reflected this concern. "Just talk to them. I know that you enunciate words, but you have to let them flow together and be a regular person." In this prosecutor's view, the opening statement's emphatic delivery distanced its author from her lay audience. Another lawyer also thought this opening statement was "too dramatic" at the beginning but that the story improved as its deliverer "calmed down" and spoke "naturally."

In cases with ambiguous evidence, prosecutors generally erred on the side of understatement, weighing the benefit of emphatic claims against jurors' imagined skepticism and defense counsel's imagined counterarguments. In a wire fraud case, for example, a supervisor implored the deliverer of an opening statement not to characterize a defendant's confession as "the most devastating evidence of all." Since the defendant did not concede that he lied to the victim or committed wire fraud, the supervisor advised the trial team to proceed with caution. "When I hear confession," he explained, "I'm thinking 'I robbed the bank. I aimed the gun at the bank teller.' *That's* a confession, and *this* is a little different."

Language or visual aids perceived as exaggerating or overstating evidence were criticized along similar lines. One prosecutor's discomfort with the practice of displaying photographs prompted her to refer to their inclusion as turning an opening statement into a "dog and pony show," while another commented that if they were going to be used as evidence of physical injuries, photographs should have a "blockbuster" effect on the jury—or not be used at all. Another response to the opening for the mortgage fraud case described at the start of this chapter also illustrates this point: "I would also be careful about overcommitting to evidence. You say 60 to 80 percent of mortgages, but you don't know he'll testify to that. I'd say 'majority' or something squishier." This sense of the value of exact language was shared by a prosecutor who cautioned the deliverer of another opening statement not to set jurors up to expect something "huge and earth-shattering" that might not be perceived as such. Another prosecutor told a colleague that he sounded as though he was welcoming jurors to the greatest show on earth when, in fact, he was setting the stage for a police officer to testify about records he analyzed. During the same meeting, a prosecutor advised another colleague not to "bomb-throw" after a peer suggested the opening line should grab the jurors "by the scruff of their neck."

The creative and imaginative labor that prosecutors devoted to reformulating case stories illuminated their divergent ideas about the relationship between advocacy and professionalism. Neither "overzealousness" nor the obligation to serve as "ministers of justice" is explicitly defined under the ethics rules governing prosecutors' conduct, and so reference to hypothetical jurors created an opening for prosecutors to bring distinct understandings of their professional responsibilities (however aspirational) to critiques of colleagues' work.

Reflecting on the role of lay decision makers during case preparation, a prosecutor explained that "the jury forces us to really think about whether we *should* do something that we *can* do in terms of a case." As this chapter suggests, the "should" of justice does not assume a singular or stable form. Conceptions of the just prosecutor—and just prosecution—are rehashed and reformulated as trial narratives take shape. Through references to jurors' perspectives, prosecutors explained their professional commitments to each other and to themselves. In the process of commenting on evidence and witnesses and developing their authorial voices, prosecutors explicitly and implicitly articulated character traits and values they viewed as central to their jobs.

Attention to legal storytelling in real time offers a corrective to studies that treat prosecutors, legal language, or law more broadly as monolithic. Research methods that rely on post hoc interviews or surveys can exacerbate this problem by failing to capture moments of disagreement or indeterminacy in real time.[9] In retrospect, even decisions fraught with ambiguity can appear to be coherent products of consensus. The social process by which the prosecutors I observed created and revised opening statement narratives, however, brings to light the contingency of their work. This process of prosecutors scrutinizing their professional identities and character through jurors' eyes also offers a window into the vital role lay knowledge plays in the exercise of discretion. Ordinary citizens, both real and imagined, were tied to the creative and collaborative process of pursuing justice.

4

Self-Conscious Voir Dire

When any large and identifiable segment of the community is excluded from jury service, the effect is to remove from the jury room qualities of human nature and varieties of human experience, the range of which is unknown and perhaps unknowable. It is not necessary to assume that the excluded group will consistently vote as a class in order to conclude, as we do, that its exclusion deprives the jury of a perspective on human events that may have unsuspected importance in any case that may be presented.
—Justice Thurgood Marshall, *Peters v. Kiff* (1972)

It was the second day of jury selection in a fraud prosecution. The government had four remaining peremptory strikes it could use to excuse jurors. A white man with unkempt gray hair entered the courtroom and took a seat in the first row of the empty jury box. When the trial team had "parsed" his questionnaire the previous weekend, a few things stood out. First, the man said he was retired from city government and might recognize the faces of people on the witness list. Second, when asked whether a personal hardship might preclude him from serving, he described plans to renovate his basement. The trial team had agreed that they could not excuse this prospective juror for cause, so he returned to court for questioning.

As the judge addressed him, one of the prosecutors leaned toward me, cell phone in hand. He had looked up the name of a website that the man had listed as a source of news and presented me with a Wikipedia page about it. It was a neo-Nazi forum. My stomach turned. In a courtroom filled with reporters, would a white supremacist be empaneled as a juror?

The lead prosecutor argued vehemently that the judge should excuse him. A person who regularly visits a racist website cannot be fair and impartial, he said. An attorney for one of the defendants responded with equal passion: the juror repeatedly *said* he could be fair. If anyone was biased, he argued, it was the government. Why not consider "all sides" of the news?

The judge left the gray-haired man on the jury, and the trial team's deliberation continued in whispers. Prior to this revelation, the prosecutors had not planned to strike him. Should they excuse a librarian who had read about the case instead? Should the government remove him during the next round of peremptory strikes? And then there was an ever-unsettling reality: it was impossible to predict what they might learn about the people they would question next.

The only time the AUSAs I observed typically discussed race and racism was during jury selection. It was a topic that could not be avoided in this region: the area around the US attorney's office was known for its racial divisions in terms of access to housing, education, and social inequality more generally. But prosecutors did not raise the issue of race because of their interest in these broader social facts. Rather, they were preoccupied with the idea that they might be challenged, on the record, for illegally dismissing prospective jurors *based on race*. If jury trials were rare, these challenges—called "*Batson* challenges," after the Supreme Court case that helped create them—were far rarer still, surfacing in only a few cases among those that actually went to trial. Yet, like the gaze of potential jurors, the specter of such scrutiny prompted meticulous preparation by the AUSAs.

I noted that prosecutors tended to demonstrate their sensitivity to race-based jury exclusion in court by recording the race of prospective jurors as they were questioned by the judge. But in an environment in which courtroom norms and antidiscrimination law under *Batson v. Kentucky* (1986) dictated that race *not* factor into lawyers' empanelment of jurors, some felt uneasy about this practice. "Many attorneys find it stressful to keep track of race for fear of being perceived as racist," a prosecutor commented in her office one morning as we talked about her approach to picking a jury in a recent carjacking case. A colleague, meanwhile, emphasized his frustration that he could not explicitly ask jurors to identify their own racial or ethnic backgrounds. "One crazy thing I noticed," he told me, "is that jury questionnaires don't ask people to self-identify." Making inaccurate assumptions about a person's race, he explained, could prompt colleagues to question his judgment or motivations for excusing jurors. And in some cases, prosecutors' conversations with defense counsel highlighted their sensitivity to the problem of even appearing to disparately strike potential jurors who were Black. During a break in jury selection proceedings, for example, a defense attorney joked with the lead prosecutor that his adversary would "look like a racist piece of shit" if he excused any one of the Black jurors in the group.

It might strike the casual observer as odd that in a criminal prosecution, the first people to face judgment are ordinary citizens, not the defendant. Though trials offered prosecutors the opportunity to work with actual jurors, the inner thoughts of these lay decision makers remained a subject of speculation. Anxiety about the effects of such speculation were compounded by the speed of the process. Most judges conducted voir dire so hastily that after they read a generic jury questionnaire aloud to the first juror, they encouraged the rest of the venire, or prospective jury panel, to respond only with reference to the question number followed by a brief response. It was routine, for example, for jurors to respond to a question like "What is your occupation?" and "How long have you held this position?" with "One: Third grade teacher. Two: Eighteen years," and so on, producing a string of disconnected facts. Based on jurors' answers to these questions, judges and lawyers could choose to dismiss them from service using one of two techniques: a "cause" challenge, exercised by judges, or a peremptory strike, exercised by the prosecutors and defense attorneys. Prosecutors usually had six peremptory strikes at their disposal, while the defense typically had ten.

In writing on both methods of juror dismissal, sociolegal scholars have examined the significant openings they create for racial and socioeconomic exclusion, facilitated in large part by the nontransparent decision-making processes that support them.[1] Building on this literature, ethnographic research offers a different kind of window into practices of juror assessment, focusing on how prosecutors make strike decisions in a manner that reflects their acute self-consciousness about how these decisions might affect the way that others, including jurors, perceive them. Antidiscrimination norms aimed at reinforcing values of inclusivity and eschewing reliance on racial stereotypes thus change the way prosecutors pick juries.

In the process of assessing the information shared by jurors, prosecutors gave voice to the ethos they knew *ought* to guide their approach to voir dire. Recognizing the reputational harm that could be accompanied by a challenge to their compliance with *Batson v. Kentucky*, a practical consequence of this self-consciousness about race during jury selection was the active effort many prosecutors made to empanel prospective jurors of color. Prosecutors' conversations with one another about these decisions, along with the unprompted commentaries they shared with each other (and with me) during breaks in proceedings, offered further evidence of how they understood jurors and of the extent to which they believed their approaches to jury empanelment reflected (or failed to reflect) their professional integrity.

The Specter of a *Batson* Challenge

Peremptory strikes presented an opportunity for prosecutors to explicitly consider the ethics of assessing jurors. Prosecutors were certainly aware of the reputational harm that could follow from being accused of excluding a prospective juror based on race or sex. The case that outlined such constitutional protections—along with a procedure for challenging a prejudicial juror dismissal—was *Batson v. Kentucky*, which prohibited the excusal of jurors based on membership in a protected class. In an innovative move that departed from precedent, the case authorized judges to scrutinize prosecutors' rationales for striking jurors in the context of a single trial and furnished lawyers with a new tool— the *Batson* challenge—that could be directed toward an adversary whose strike constituted a prima facie case of discrimination.[2]

The familiarity of the prosecutors with *Batson* was reinforced by the office's organization of a continuing legal education presentation on the subject, which was accompanied by PowerPoint slides that some trial teams brought with them to the courtroom for reference. Critics of the *Batson* framework have rightly highlighted its limited capacity to identify prosecutors who are "of a mind" to exclude jurors of color or to deter them from doing so.[3] Scholars have noted that if they are asked to account for their peremptory strike decisions after a *Batson* challenge, prosecutors can easily conceal prejudicial motives by offering pretextual or post hoc rationales for their decisions.[4] Without the means to definitively test the veracity of their strike rationales, *Batson*'s "race-neutral" aspiration, by these accounts, is impracticable.[5] Despite the widely recognized limitations of *Batson*, which have been the subject of voluminous legal scholarship, ethnographic research reveals that the doctrine has in fact changed lawyers' jury selection strategies.

This finding builds on other qualitative research showing a link between the antidiscrimination norms embodied by *Batson* and lawyers' approaches to picking juries. A qualitative case study of the Midwest, for example, revealed that while most attorneys rely on race, gender, and class stereotypes during jury selection, *Batson* has led to increased awareness of the importance of seeking an inclusive jury.[6] In line with this, the research I analyze here indicates that reforming voir dire to achieve race-neutral jury selection has kept race at the forefront of prosecutors' thinking.

Beyond Race Neutrality

Accounts offered by the prosecutors I observed of their experiences anticipating and navigating *Batson* challenges revealed the centrality of racial information to their assessments of jurors. The prosecutors I interviewed all agreed first and foremost that jurors' attitudes toward cases were inherently unpredictable.[7] Prosecutors lamented the lack of useful information elicited from jurors during voir dire and recognized that regardless of their own efforts, jury verdicts in criminal cases could be idiosyncratic.[8] On top of that, judges in the district routinely delineated the scope of relevant questioning themselves and often posed questions to prospective jurors without opportunities for attorney-led follow-up. These generally standardized inquiries were supplemented by case-specific questions submitted by the attorneys along with follow-up questioning at sidebar facilitated by the judge.[9] As a result, prosecutors found themselves assessing the strangers who reported for jury service based on scanty information, aided by largely routinized, yes-or-no questions.[10] Variations in individual judges' management of jury selection made the process only more uncertain. Although judge-led voir dire is more common in federal court, judges also tend to be actively involved in state voir dire proceedings.[11]

Outside the courtroom, prosecutors discovered—through continuing legal education classes, meetings with supervisors, and anecdotes from colleagues—that *Batson* challenges were among the most significant disputes one could face during jury selection. This became a risk, prosecutors learned, if they excused Black or female prospective jurors from their cases. Though uncommon in practice, the adjudication of *Batson* challenges represented a frequent source of anxiety for the attorneys I observed. This anxiety imprinted itself on their approaches to jury selection.[12]

Making Race and Gender Salient

An AUSA once said to me that when jurors first enter a courtroom, they have nothing to do. As a result, he explained, they scrutinize prosecutors' every move, word, facial expression, and nervous tick. Picking a jury is, as he put it, "fucking exhausting." Prosecutors readily and repeatedly shared thoughts on jury selection to this effect, revealing their sensitivity to jurors' seemingly limitless attention to their speech, behavior, and even dress.[13] Prosecutors were especially concerned about how their decisions to excuse particular jurors might affect others' perceptions of their motivations, biases, and credibility as attorneys. They might be seen as untrustworthy, slick, abrasive, overbearing, condescending, or arrogant. Any of that would be bad—though not as bad as being seen as that one thing they wished to avoid above everything else: *racist*.

In some cases, prosecutors addressed this anxiety by refraining from using peremptory strikes altogether. Instead, these prosecutors embraced an inclusive jury selection strategy—referred to by some as the "first twelve in the box" approach.[14] According to this approach, prospective jurors' responses were viewed as irrelevant. One critical test of the strength of a prosecutor's case, some thought, was a lawyer's willingness to empanel *any* eligible juror.[15] Such prosecutors believed this method conveyed confidence in their cases and evidence while eliminating the possibility of having assessments of jurors scrutinized.

Beyond worrying about whether to use peremptory strikes, prosecutors also registered concern when discussing the criticism they might face for particular strike decisions. Some prosecutors I spoke with were explicitly trained through the office's continuing legal education classes to understand they had a legal responsibility to keep considerations of race, gender, and religious affiliation out of their assessments of jurors. Yet in a low-information environment, the very characteristics that prosecutors were not permitted to consider became essential heuristics for record-keeping and discussions of prospective jurors.[16] In other words, inferences about jury psychology often rested on minor aspects of jurors' identities.

Though dependent on these heuristics, some prosecutors were nevertheless so concerned that a *Batson* challenge would effectively brand them as racist in court that they developed comprehensive lists of jurors' responses that could be used to legitimize disqualification. Thus, if prosecutors were later questioned about their decisions to peremptorily challenge jurors, they would have unobjectionable explanations at hand. A goal in taking notes on jurors, as one prosecutor explained it, was therefore to "make sure you kept a good enough record so that if you got a challenge, two years later on appeal you could say I didn't strike that person because of race or gender—but here are six facts I wrote down on paper that say why I didn't like a person."

Other prosecutors felt that considerations of race were best avoided because they might obscure information more relevant to their cases. One prosecutor shared a story about a case in which his trial partner was fixated on the possibility of a *Batson* challenge as they moved through voir dire. Both prosecutors opposed striking one potential juror but for two very different reasons. The prosecutor who told me the story liked that the potential juror was a nurse, which he thought meant she would know how to "call bullshit" on the defendant, a doctor, and be able to draw on her professional experience to substantiate her views. His trial partner, by contrast, wanted to keep the potential juror because she was a Hispanic woman of similar age and background to the defendant. For this prosecutor, the nurse's inclusion in the pool was important not only because of her knowledge and perspective but also because of the *Batson* challenge that might ensue if she were dismissed.

If prosecutors feared being the target of a challenge, many also felt uneasy about targeting others. One civil division attorney, who defended a federal agency in an employment discrimination case, for example, considered challenging the plaintiff for dismissing a Hispanic man from the jury pool. He ultimately decided against it. "If I had challenged him," he recalled, "the plaintiff could have come up with a nondiscriminatory reason. But would I offend the jury? Would they hear this? They *shouldn't* hear this, but who knows. And maybe the judge would not be happy with plaintiff's counsel." In this case, the lawyer worried about the effect that an uncertain and unpredictable *Batson* challenge could have on the rest of the venire.

Prosecutors' personal experience of prejudice and racism also influenced how they exercised *Batson* challenges in *response* to defense counsel's conduct. One prosecutor noted, for example, that as a "minority prosecutor" he was particularly interested in ensuring that jury selection proceedings were inclusive and that juries were representative. He explained that there were not many federal practitioners of color in the district, a fact that made him all the more cognizant of whether he used his strikes or the defense used theirs against people of color. This prosecutor's experience of practicing law in the district was defined by his attention to the demographics of colleagues, adversaries, and jurors, and so he valued the chance *Batson* gave him to hold defense counsel accountable if he perceived them to be using exclusionary tactics to influence the demographics of a jury pool.

Other prosecutors refrained from using peremptory strikes out of concern that even an unfounded *Batson* challenge could be a source of humiliation or embarrassment. Fear of being labeled as racist was a significant deterrent for such prosecutors, who chose to direct their attention to other aspects of trial preparation. In other cases, concern about being viewed as racist prompted prosecutors to avoid striking jurors altogether. Despite identifying "huge red flags" in certain jurors' responses to questions—and particularly those related to their contact with law enforcement—a prosecutor reflected that "unless you can articulate a bias" on the part of such a juror, striking him or her is out of the question. She reflected that sometimes she had a "gut feeling" about certain jurors that was conveyed through their "body language": "Some of it is not so much what they're saying as *reading* them. . . . It's just kind of sometimes you have a feeling that lady will be pissed she's here, pissed she has to sit through this, and will hold it against us." The prosecutor added, however, that if the prospective juror is a person of color in an otherwise racially homogeneous venire, then the race of such a juror should weigh heavily in deciding whether to strike her.

Another prosecutor described leaving an office-wide continuing legal education presentation on jury selection feeling so "scared" she might be challenged for dismissing a juror for "legal and appropriate" reasons that she did not want to risk confrontation. For this reason, she, too, was reluctant to challenge jurors at all. Another prosecutor's self-consciousness left her feeling limited to striking white jurors when she was faced with a predominantly white venire.

Prosecutors' self-conscious attention to the sex of prospective jurors exhibited similar patterns. On some occasions, prosecutors' concerns about the personal and reputational stakes of potential *Batson* challenges led them to deliberately excuse female prospective jurors. In a rape case I observed, the members of the trial team worried about the fact that all the prospective jurors on their strike list were men, and so they anxiously revisited the notes they had taken during voir dire in the hope of identifying women they could justify excusing. They discovered in the process that one female prospective juror had referred to herself as "kooky" and "out there" and that another had noted that her daughter had once been a victim of sexual assault. Though both women believed they could be fair jurors, the prosecutors decided to strike them out of concern they could otherwise face a *Batson* challenge for striking too many men. If not for this *Batson*-related concern, one member of the trial team explained, they would unquestionably have left these prospective jurors alone, since neither of them had initially raised suspicion.

This approach was not shared by all. Others were skeptical of assessments that took a juror's sex into account. In some cases, their views stemmed from past trial experiences. Citing a case in which a suit was brought against the government by a female plaintiff who had breast cancer, for example, a civil division attorney explained that his "knee-jerk" reaction had been to avoid empaneling female jurors on the theory they might sympathize with the plaintiff. Conversations with colleagues, however, convinced him that his intuitions were off base under the circumstances. He explained that others who had tried these types of cases felt they did "better" with female jurors because women expected other women to "take some responsibility and look out for themselves" to a greater extent than men did. He therefore credited his sense of the irrelevance of gender considerations to colleagues' case experience and not to concern about *Batson*.

Another common explanation prosecutors offered for considering the race or sex of a prospective juror was a strategic one: recording these characteristics was essential to defending oneself in the adjudication of a *Batson* challenge, should it arise. Prosecutors worried that if they *failed* to explicitly assign racial identities to jurors, they might unwittingly break the law if their decisions were challenged. And the same might be true of judges. The possibility of an appeal might lead them to pay special attention to—and often record—the racial identities of jurors they excused from their courtrooms.[17]

Despite succumbing to supervisors' and colleagues' pressure to preemptively classify prospective jurors along racial lines, some prosecutors still commented on the paradox of feeling analytically dependent on the characteristics they were not legally meant to consider. One prosecutor explained that "from a policy standpoint," *Batson* in fact reinforced the classifications it was designed to eliminate. "It's supposed to prevent you from taking race into account," he said, "but in fact makes you think of it more."

Several other prosecutors made the same observation, noting that their familiarity with *Batson* made them only more attuned to race during jury selection. Since jurors were not asked to specify their own racial identities, however, these designations required guesswork. In many cases, the racial identities of prospective jurors were ambiguous to prosecutors. During jury selection proceedings in one case, for example, a prosecutor asked a colleague whether to identify a particular juror as Dominican. In another case, a prosecutor commented that she was trying to locate references to a prospective juror whom she recalled identifying as Hispanic. This challenge of assigning broad racial categories was compounded by the fact that judges sometimes identified prospective jurors differently.[18]

During jury selection in one criminal case, a lead prosecutor and her colleague disagreed about the appropriateness of recording racial information about prospective jurors. The lead prosecutor insisted that like many of her colleagues, she should "keep track of race" as a *Batson* challenge contingency plan, while her colleague opposed that strategy.

Another prosecutor took the same view: in one case, she had made sure to note that a favorite potential juror of hers was Black in the event she was later accused of bringing racial animus to her assessments of jurors. The empanelment of some Black jurors, in her view, undermined possible claims that she had wrongfully excluded others.

In other jury selection proceedings that involved written questionnaires that trial teams could review in advance, the presumed racial identities of prospective jurors were appended to lists of issues that were flagged for follow-up in case these jurors were subject to future peremptory strikes. In one case, a trial team struggled with the fact that a Black prospective juror said she did not find children to be reliable witnesses. After a supervisor told the prosecutors to anticipate a *Batson* challenge if any Black prospective juror was struck, they cautiously revisited the juror's responses to other questions. The trial team worried that legitimate concerns about the juror might not withstand later scrutiny and wondered if the juror's troubling responses to other questions would aid their defense. Exasperated by this exercise, a member of the trial team lamented the fact that racial identifications should enter their deliberations at all. His colleague, however, urged caution, recognizing the seriousness of a challenge by defense counsel.

Prosecutors often weighed problematic juror responses against the possibility of a *Batson* challenge that would lead to the public and humiliating scrutiny of juror dismissals. Overall, my ethnographic research suggests that the specter of a *Batson* challenge affects trial processes, decision-making, and everything from notetaking practices to rationales for strike-targeting. Prosecutors considered both their in-court, case-specific reputations—winning a case before a jury is much easier if the jury does not think you are racist or sexist—and their broader professional reputations.[19] Beyond instrumental concerns about the possibility of later appeal, the negative valence of racism and sexism in American society at large, coupled with public scrutiny of jury exclusion, heightened prosecutors' desire to avoid patterns of professional behavior indicative of animus toward particular groups. A *Batson* challenge was thus not just a procedural issue for many prosecutors but also a personal one.

Inclusion in *Batson*'s Name

To avoid the stigma associated with an accusation of harboring racial animus, several federal prosecutors made a concerted effort to empanel Black jurors and challenge white jurors whenever possible. As a matter of intra-unit policy, one prosecutor recalled being told by a supervisor that if there was one Black prospective juror in the venire, prosecutors should refrain from excusing him or her in the absence of extenuating circumstances. It struck this prosecutor as strange that his colleagues' approaches to jury selection appeared to necessitate racial distinctions rather than diminish them.

This strategy sometimes resulted in the inclusion of jurors whose responses during voir dire worried prosecutors. One such juror left the courtroom in the middle of a bank robbery trial without explanation. In another case, a juror who was empaneled denied having negative feelings toward a law enforcement officer *who killed a member of his family*—a response the trial team found very hard to believe. For others, the race-consciousness introduced by concern about *Batson* challenges led them to seek Black jurors in prosecutions of Black defendants.

A related consequence of this race-conscious orientation was prosecutors' willingness to dismiss otherwise eligible and unobjectionable white prospective jurors. In one case, a man who commented during one-on-one questioning that he was concerned that a prosecutor could manipulate a cooperating witness was struck. Though the trial team felt they could easily have rehabilitated the juror, they had no qualms about moving the juror "up" on their strike list, noting defense counsel would be indifferent if they "struck a white guy."

Prosecutors also explicitly referenced prospective jurors' racial identities when revisiting notes to confirm they had been consistent in the way they discussed "analogous" jurors. For example, they flagged for commensurate follow-up questioning *all* jurors who said they had voted to acquit defendants as jurors in past cases.

In some cases, prosecutors' self-consciousness about potential *Batson* challenges showed how they often acted on their own biases. Once, thinking about gender, a prosecutor said she regularly considered a prospective juror's "gender combined with age." She worried that in cases with a "thirty- to thirty-five-year-old male defendant of any race," a young female juror might feel attracted to him and unduly sympathetic. She explained that such defendants could appear to be the "strong, silent type." "He's a little risqué and a little interesting and he's a little cute sitting there," she commented, imagining how a young woman might regard such a defendant. Under these circumstances, the prosecutor felt it was necessary to strike young women. Other female prosecutors excused women from juries out of concern that such jurors might judge *them* or view them competitively. Where some prosecutors embraced *Batson*'s deterrent effect on legally impermissible considerations, others readily embraced stereotypes that excluded women from jury service.

Concern about potential *Batson* challenges also led prosecutors to scrutinize whether strike decisions based on seemingly innocuous grounds might be viewed as "proxies" for race. Prosecutors worried, for example, about the implications of a routine question that was asked of jurors in federal court related to whether they owned or rented their home. It struck some prosecutors as problematic that homeowners were conventionally viewed as more likely than renters to condemn criminal activity that might adversely affect the value of their property, which implied they had a more significant stake in their communities. If jurors' responses to this question led to the dismissal of one or two prospective jurors of color, a prosecutor explained, he expected to hear defense counsel accuse him of "coming up with excuses" to empanel white jurors who were more likely to own their homes. Another prosecutor struggled with his inclination to empanel jurors who said they trusted police officers in light of his understanding of the relationship between race, mass incarceration, and skepticism toward law enforcement. Everything he knew to be true based on research, he explained, he was not "allowed to consider and take into account."

In some cases, prosecutors' apprehension about potential challenges led them to misapply the law by supplying rationales for their strikes to preempt judges' determinations of whether a prima facie case of discrimination had been made by the challenging party. Though in principle prosecutors are only called upon to offer explanations for strikes *after* judges have made such a finding, the gap between principle and practice was on full display during voir dire. Prosecutors were sometimes so distressed by *Batson* challenges threatened or made against them that they rushed to offer "neutral" reasons for their strikes. One prosecutor speculated that her colleagues' eagerness to prematurely offer reasons for dismissing jurors stemmed from the unsettling experience of having their integrity questioned. When "called a racist," she explained, a prosecutor naturally felt compelled to defend herself. Other prosecutors noted feeling "indignant" and "emotional" when challenged.

These findings on the link between consciousness of the race and sex of jurors and professional and personal considerations support conclusions drawn elsewhere. One interview-based study, for example, documents the extent to which the prosecutors who were the subject of the study internalized antidiscrimination norms in their approaches to voir dire and notes that even the *possibility* of a *Batson* challenge had an "educating effect" on lawyers' thinking.[20] This study also highlights the stigmatizing potential of the law. One prosecutor "reported being so upset at a lengthy *Batson* hearing out of the jury's presence as to ask, 'Judge, are you going to brand me as a racist because I exercised a peremptory?' and was mildly rebuked by the court"; another noted that he tried not—and "not just because of *Batson*"—"to let race influence [his] decision about jurors"; yet another "did not recall a prosecutor ever removing an African American juror on voir dire."

My ethnographic research shows what this educating effect entailed and compelled in practice, namely, an explicit link between anticipation of *Batson* challenges or violations and a race-conscious approach to the jury selection process. This approach involved scrupulously collecting demographic data that could lead prosecutors to make empanelment decisions motivated by concern about how they might be perceived by others.

Sparing the Burdened Juror

Race, ethnicity, and sex were not the only characteristics of prospective jurors prosecutors considered—class was another. During jury selection proceedings in a white-collar case, defense counsel raised a *Batson* challenge after prosecutors dismissed a woman who said, among other things, that she did not have hobbies and that her mother worked in a factory for a company that she could not recall the name of. In response to the prosecutors' use of a peremptory strike to excuse the juror, defense counsel argued that the government's stated rationales were proxies for its desire to excuse her because she was Hispanic. The prosecutors denied that the juror's ethnicity prompted her excusal, and indeed, this was not the first time I saw prosecutors strike prospective jurors whose occupations, life experience, or lack of discretionary time were indicative of financial struggles. Prosecutors often justified such excusals on the grounds that because they were the party responsible for bringing criminal cases to court, they could end up being perceived by others, including jurors, as creating an additional and undue burden by empaneling jurors whose time might be better spent working to support their families.

Efforts to excuse prospective jurors based on financial hardship during the "cause challenge" phase of jury selection proceedings thus presented another arena in which prosecutors saw their jury selection strategies as potentially signaling something about themselves. Judges exercise cause challenges—distinct from the peremptory strikes that attorneys can make that are limited in number and constrained only by antidiscrimination law—and can do so for a variety of reasons.[21] Excusing jurors who indicate that financial constraints prevent them from participating is one such reason.[22] But the judges I observed were sometimes loath to lose jurors on account of employment challenges that were likely to be shared by all. It did not help that financial hardship was ambiguously and subjectively defined.[23] The judges I observed were also reluctant to honor juror excuses that could lead to the loss of a venire, or a "busted panel," as some called it. This led some judges to opt to listen to hardship claims in private sidebar interactions rather than in open court. Judges who were parsimonious in their excusal of jurors could thus move through the jury selection process quickly, which some prosecutors preferred.

A consequence of many judges' reluctance to excuse prospective jurors for cause was that they ended up conveying the sense that they were indifferent to the financial struggles of laypeople in the district. On several occasions, I watched judges ignore or treat as irrelevant the fact that a prospective juror's job required working night shifts. One judge, for example, reasoned that night shifts would not conflict with the trial schedule. I also saw judges operate under the fiction that shift workers would receive paychecks despite missing work. Other judges showed disregard for prospective jurors' lack of access to cars or public transportation.

Insofar as jurors' onerous caretaking responsibilities fell outside of the trial schedule, they, too, were invisible. Only in response to the rare detailed jury questionnaires could lawyers see glimmers of jurors' struggles to support themselves due to precarious or part-time employment, children or relatives who required care, or illnesses. Still, in the case of written questionnaires, answers were sometimes unintelligible, left blank, or marked "private" or "N/A."

Although cause challenges theoretically lay within the sole discretion of the court, in practice these decisions were often deferred to prosecutors and defense attorneys. Some prosecutors viewed judges' willingness to pass the buck on hardship excuses as problematic, but others welcomed the opportunity to make these judgments. It offered an opportunity for prosecutors to show benevolence and sensitivity to the idealized ordinary people on whom they relied.

Prosecutors therefore often claimed for themselves the task of assessing or speculating about the extent of a juror's financial hardship. At times, their conclusions were based on jurors' reports of conflicting professional or family commitments, while on other occasions they were based on independent appraisals of the likelihood that a juror's daily appearance in court could constitute a legitimate economic burden. Making subjective decisions about such jurors was further complicated by the convergence of an ill-defined and inconsistently deployed threshold for personal hardship.[24]

As a result, prosecutors typically worked to identify, evaluate, and contest indices of jurors' ability to serve based on the limited information provided in court, deciding among themselves what an undue financial hardship looked like, in the interest of showing compassion to people who may have felt they could not complain. Indeed, even when judges told prospective jurors that a trial could last for weeks or months, many refrained from expressing concern about losing income or jobs or about accumulating debt. Though some came forward with hardship excuses related to work constraints, childcare commitments, and worries about paying bills in light of lost income, many remained silent. Prospective jurors who responded to written questionnaires were likewise reluctant at times to characterize their personal circumstances as "extraordinary," perhaps because they recognized that many of their peers no doubt faced similar barriers to service.

Prosecutors frequently drew conclusions about jurors' abilities to serve based on their stated occupations or employers. I observed prosecutors worry aloud about a T.J.Maxx retail associate, auto repairmen, Walmart employees, a sheet metal journeyman, food service workers, warehouse shipping clerks, crossing guards, Uber drivers, substitute or assistant teachers, a produce clerk, substation mechanics, and delivery drivers. They also expressed concern about the impact of jury service on those who were unemployed but actively searching for work. One such juror had scheduled an interview that conflicted with parts of the trial. Given the juror's family responsibilities, the trial team concluded that the juror might be desperate for the job.

In other cases, prosecutors speculated about jurors' job security and work conditions. One prosecutor commented, for example, that a Williams Sonoma employee might face financial repercussions for serving as a juror because she likely worked on commission. In another case, a trial team worried that a camp director who failed to raise hardship concerns would undoubtedly suffer if the trial went through the summer. Though judges' and prosecutors' appraisals of such jurors may have been off base, most articulated an interest in sparing those who might otherwise lose shifts or wages.

When it came to prospective jurors who *did* voice concern about being empaneled for a case, prosecutors were largely unified in the belief they should not be forced to serve. Prosecutors did not want to be perceived by judges, defense counsel, or jurors as placing additional strain on people who said they could not afford the cost of day care, or worked day and night to support extended family. They did not want to appear callous or aloof, in other words, when faced with evidence of prospective jurors' struggles. Another worry was the possibility that a juror's financial hardship could lead him or her to drop out later or lose focus during the trial. These considerations sometimes led prosecutors to use their limited peremptory strikes to excuse jurors whom judges might have seated. Prosecutors' explicitly sympathetic orientation toward prospective jurors came into relief when they were confronted with jurors they perceived as *illegitimately* raising hardship claims, such as a hedge fund employee who the AUSAs felt made a "bullshit" excuse.

Prosecutors' consideration of prospective jurors' racial identities and material constraints had concrete effects on how they empaneled juries—

though not in a uniform or predictable manner. For many, attention to race and class stemmed from self-conscious concern about the repercussions of a possible *Batson* challenge or the perception that struggling jurors were coerced to participate in trials: Others were guided by more practical concerns, including the extent to which prosecutors' neglect of racial considerations could put them at a disadvantage. To address this concern, some prosecutors asked judges to include supplemental voir dire questions designed to root out prejudice in their potential lay decision makers. Though judges and defense attorneys did not always honor these requests, nearly all the prosecutors I interviewed submitted a question addressing whether prospective jurors had personal feelings about "members of any ethnic or racial group" that would make it difficult for them to be fair.[25] One prosecutor expressed frustration that jury selection—which was supposed to be "race-neutral"—nonetheless featured an explicit question about race. "Internally I wanted to fight it," the prosecutor told me, "but I took a step back, and we ultimately let the judge ask the question." He resigned himself to the inquiry, acknowledging that he would rather see a defendant convicted on the strength of his evidence than on the basis of a juror's prejudice.[26]

Other prosecutors welcomed the opportunity to discuss race out in the open. One prosecutor, for example, said that if antidiscrimination norms were reinforced during voir dire, jurors might be less likely to tolerate racist sentiments that were expressed during their deliberation. Still others were eager to elicit evidence of jurors' prejudicial attitudes toward them. Since lawyers were no less vulnerable to racist ideation, prosecutors worried *they* might be targets of discrimination. When a prospective juror responded affirmatively to a question related to racial prejudice, for example, a prosecutor was shocked: "Is she serious? She's got to be kidding. Well that isn't good for me. The judge excused her because she doesn't like Black people!"

5

Judging Character

It is not true, as some writers assume in their treatises on rhetoric, that the personal goodness revealed by the speaker contributes nothing to his power of persuasion; on the contrary, his character may almost be called the most effective means of persuasion he possesses.
—Aristotle, *The Art of Rhetoric*

Building a positive reputation in the office was not just about being competent and trying cases. One young and jovial prosecutor, for instance, was beloved by colleagues for gently mocking his supervisors in their presence. He was also considered very funny. Once, I found him sitting in the conference room with a pen in one hand and a snack bar in the other. He and his trial partner were in the process of reading jury questionnaires. After a few minutes of chewing and muttering, he abruptly stopped and let his palm fall across the top crease of a questionnaire where the pages had been stapled. The prospective juror had written that they listened to a particular sports talk show—a show that this prosecutor happened to despise.

"I'm going to write 'negative,'" he announced, penning a margin note on a Post-it. "I hate this person. I hate this show."

His trial partner chuckled over his own pile of annotated packets and confirmed that he was not a fan of the show either. Perhaps encouraged by the amusement of his colleague, the young prosecutor—who was now leaning back in his chair—proceeded with a monologue. He said the prospective juror reminded him of one of his own family members who would likely sympathize with the defendant. The prosecutor began to imagine aloud what kind of person this prospective juror is.

"I'm going to get into my big Suburban," the young prosecutor declared, as if he were the person, "and drive over to Dick's and buy another one of those lacrosse nets that I have all over my yard for my huge dog." Over the now-raucous laughter of his colleague, he continued, "Oh, climate change? What a bunch of horseshit! Have you tried any of these beers?" Ending the impression, he reaffirmed his decision to move for the person's dismissal. "I don't want that guy on my jury. Fuck *you* juror number 139!"

The young prosecutor's assessment of this juror was not atypical in an office where I witnessed AUSAs come to impulsive but surprisingly detailed—and unequivocal—conclusions about people. From a stated preference for a certain sports radio show, for example, an AUSA could sketch the personality and biography of an imagined juror, finding reason to praise or, as in this case, condemn and ultimately urge their dismissal from court. As I would learn in the office, the work of federal prosecution, particularly before and during voir dire, often revolved around this process and the question of how to judge—and prepare jurors to judge—the character of others.

Character Evidence on Trial

The American criminal trial is, in a sense, a collective exercise in assessing character.[1] From seeing *crooked* politicians and *greedy* white-collar criminals to noting *shifty* thieves and *unfeeling* murderers, there is a shared process: people make sense of the actions of others by linking these actions with seemingly immutable personality traits.[2] They are not supposed to do this—at least officially. The rules of evidence, building on common law principles, aim to prevent the replacement of substantive deliberation about evidence with knee-jerk conclusions based on typifying defendants. In fact, the rules bar presentations of evidence to jurors that might lead them to infer that because a defendant committed a past unlawful act, he or she should be viewed as having the character trait of a person who should be presumed guilty.[3] Prior crime does not make someone a presumed *criminal*, the rules say. But do jurors listen? Do lawyers?

Character judgment in legal proceedings has been a dominant theme of scholarship on the criminal trial, as well as reform efforts aimed at improving it. Such efforts led to the 1975 codification of Federal Rule of Evidence 404, which formally enshrined the common-law rule banning the presentation of evidence of character to prove that a person's act on a particular occasion reflects a character trait possessed by that person.[4] Legal scholars also use the term "character evidence" interchangeably with "propensity evidence" because they recognize that laypeople will inevitably draw shorthand connections between the presumed character traits of individuals and their "propensity to act a certain way" and support prosecution on those grounds.[5] Rule 404(b) further clarifies that "evidence of a crime, wrong, or other act" is not admissible at trial to prove conduct in conformity with any character trait that is presumed on the basis of this evidence.[6] The rule declares that propensity arguments be based only on a witness's "truthfulness."

Still, there is the open empirical question of how people—both professional legal actors and laypeople—actually attempt to assess the truthfulness of strangers, be they prospective jurors, defendants, or witnesses. One dominant mode of such evaluation, as legal scholar Julia Simon-Kerr describes it, entails relying on generalizations or stereotypes that produce coherent impressions of others' credibility. "When credibility matters," Simon-Kerr writes, "we will inevitably use such heuristics to categorize and evaluate the truth of what we are told, particularly by those about whom we have little personal knowledge."[7]

But judging credibility in this manner is prone to various errors. First, there is the issue of accuracy. Propensity inferences rest on the dubious assumption that because a person has engaged in a certain kind of conduct in the past, she will inevitably do so again in the future.[8] When it comes to lying, for example, it is questionable whether indulging in minor or trivial deviations from, or distortions of, the truth—"white lies," exaggerations, and embellishments—in one or more previous instances should suggest that a defendant is a *liar*, who is lying about her role in committing a crime. Writing about American politics, anthropologist Carole McGranahan has noted how lies are not all the same. They can be characterized variously as falsehoods, unsubstantiated claims, "alternative facts," and even bouts of "serial carelessness."[9] What these euphemisms reflect is the contingency of public accounts of dishonesty—contingency that is at times forgotten in the rush to determine a person's character.

Another danger that attends the routine judgment of character by federal prosecutors—and other legal actors—is the reproduction and exacerbation of racial and socioeconomic exclusion, due to the common and often tacit negative identification of certain traits and interests. One example, which I witnessed on multiple occasions, was that prosecutors infer that a person's previous negative contact with law enforcement signaled bias or unreliability as a neutral arbiter of evidence and testimony. This one fact could, in the eyes of an AUSA looking for a favorable jury, provide the basis for a character assessment that justified efforts to seek dismissal.

Even with the potential pitfalls associated with character judgment, the prosecutors I observed were aggressive collectors of what they viewed as useful character evidence—particularly during jury selection. In fact, favoring or disfavoring a prospective juror was often determined by generalizations about the person's character based on his or her responses to questions—formulated and asked by judges—such as "Have you ever had a negative experience with the state or federal government or with police that makes you distrust law enforcement officers?" or "Have you or has anyone you know, including a family member or close friend, been accused of or involved in reporting or being a victim of a crime?"

Many of the prosecutors I spoke with concluded that jurors who responded that they had had a negative experience with law enforcement would react unfavorably to any FBI agent or police officer who might testify. As one prosecutor cautioned, such jurors may "just hate cops." Another prosecutor remarked that answers to questions that probed jurors' relationships with law enforcement officers could offer a uniquely "intimate window" into people's lives, yielding accounts of personal experiences of victimization that might contribute to making them thoughtful jurors. For most, however, prospective jurors who shared the fact that they had a "bad experience with law enforcement," even if the experience they described involved family members being falsely or "continuously arrested" as a result of discriminatory policing tactics, were deemed "bad jurors."

They were "bad" in the eyes of many AUSAs even if they pledged to be impartial or declared that this negative experience would have no effect on their participation in the current trial. In one case, for instance, I witnessed a prospective juror confirm that though her father had been shot by a police officer, she would be able to "look past that" in serving as a juror. To me, the trial team stated emphatically that they did not believe her. Negative experiences, regardless of how prospective jurors claimed to have processed them, were not strike one against a person; they were, to many of the prosecutors I studied, all three strikes.

On the other hand, people who shared positive views of, or who had close relations with, police officers prompted favorable judgment. One prosecutor explained to me that despite having reservations about a prospective juror—a professor—he shared that the person "helped reassure us" when he mentioned that he respected his uncle, a police officer. Even better than someone who praised law enforcement, according to the AUSAs, was someone who had been a law enforcement agent or worked closely with one. Such prospective jurors were viewed as likely to be receptive to the government's case and were thus highly desirable.

The AUSAs were similarly enthusiastic about victims of crime, concluding that these people would favor the prosecution's case and view police officers not as oppressors but as protectors who had come to their aid or pursued the criminals who had harmed them. The clear exception to this, I learned, was victims or kin of victims of unsolved sexual assault cases. These were, apparently, bad jurors for the government. One prospective juror, for example, shared that his wife had been the victim of an attempted rape when the two were on a vacation together decades earlier. The prosecutor present urged the judge to dismiss the juror, which the judge did. People previously suspected—though not convicted—of a crime also had to go. During a different case, a sexual assault prosecution, a trial team was emphatic that anyone who had "ever been accused" of date rape or sexual assault could never be empaneled as a juror. "I'm sorry," said one of the prosecutors. "You can't be fair. I can't have someone personally accused of a sex offense."

These interpretive tendencies, though quite common among the AUSAs I observed, interviewed, and consulted in the course of my research, were not shared by all. And to give a fuller picture of their approaches to character judgment, I must mention at least one case where a prosecutor demonstrated heightened sensitivity to the fact that negative interactions with law enforcement did not necessarily make a person a "bad juror." Once, for example, an AUSA noted that while prospective jurors from one particular county often listed family members who worked in law enforcement, those from the adjacent county regularly shared accounts of being victimized by police and incarcerated.

This prosecutor emphasized that if you looked at the "data and statistics," it was clear that any character judgments that followed from these facts would likely correlate with the significant racial and socioeconomic disparities between these two counties. The individuals who would be labeled "bad jurors" in this case were disproportionately people of color who were poor.

A colleague of this prosecutor went further, cautioning against letting a "strong visceral reaction" to a person's stated antipathy toward police inform character judgment. Just because a person shared that a police officer acted wrongfully or criminally should not, this prosecutor maintained, lead one to conclude that he or she felt *all* cops do "shitty jobs." Aren't laypeople capable of nuance? Of separating what happened *then* from what is happening *now*? This prosecutor explained that he would always "ask other questions" to figure out whether the juror had an "ax to grind" or a "vendetta" that would result in disregard for the government's evidence. He did not believe that learning of negative law enforcement contact was adequate for building a useful character assessment. I think that most of the other AUSAs I studied would have disagreed.

Crafting Character for Jurors

Prospective jurors were not the only people whose character was important to prosecutors. Prosecutors also crafted entire lines of questioning for *witnesses* that aimed to evoke certain kinds of impressions that would be picked up by jurors, who they sensed would already be looking for signs of character. Because prosecutors had no access to jurors' actual impressions of witnesses, they drew on their own local knowledge and imagined how certain responses—and ways of responding—might lead jurors to draw conclusions about the witnesses' trustworthiness and integrity. This, I learned, was something many AUSAs believed was necessary to make sure that the substance of the testimony was received favorably.

Or, as the case might be, *unfavorably*. When it came to dealing with witnesses for the defense, prosecutors also made character central, working to discredit testimony by demonstrating that its source was *generally* unreliable. After all, if a witness could be shown to have lied in a variety of unrelated contexts, wouldn't a juror conclude that the witness was also likely lying on the stand? The AUSAs who pursued this strategy believed so and aimed to evoke impressions or traits that they thought jurors might associate with the cultural stereotypes of a "pathological" liar, an "ideological" religious or political zealot, or a naive and vulnerable child.

The prosecutors I observed were creative when it came to trial preparation and strategy, and they relied heavily on improvisation. Chief among their concerns as they prepared for cross-examination was the matter of how to present witnesses, as well as defendants, as untrustworthy. Prosecutors understood this task as one of narratively distinguishing the unreliable person—or *habitual* liar—from the person who might be unreliable on a particular occasion but was otherwise trustworthy.

In the course of one trial, for example, a prosecutor was anxious that a particular defendant would testify. The defendant, a professional raising several children on her own, seemed too sympathetic. As the prosecutor and her colleagues convened to prepare to question the defendant, they discussed the challenge of discrediting her in light of her apparently good character as a devoted mother. The trial team's efforts to portray her as a liar became a collective narrative project that involved carefully revisiting the defendant's communications to family, friends, and co-workers for logical inconsistencies. The image they wanted to create for the jury was one of a person willing to bend the truth for her benefit—and at the expense of others. She should come off not as a struggling caregiver but as a calculating and self-interested schemer. *That* was the kind of person jurors would see as a liar, both in and outside of the courtroom.

But how to do it? The prosecutors returned to a comment defense counsel made during opening statements in the trial. It represented the defendant as so concerned about the financial well-being of her family that she chose to take circuitous and traffic-heavy roads to avoid tolls. This statement had seemed unremarkable at the time. Upon reflection, however, the prosecutors realized that something about it rang false—it seemed implausible and too specific.

"She probably never took [the tollway] even when she wasn't trying to save money," one prosecutor stated abruptly during an evening meeting.

"She probably just threw this in for sympathy." The prosecutor added that given where the defendant worked, it actually made more sense for her to take the non-toll roads the defense had claimed were out of her way. Several AUSAs followed up with comments on the relative efficacy of respective commuting routes.

"What I'd like to get is the [toll tag] record," one said, "and show she never took the [thruway]."

Together, the prosecutors had discovered that this little statement— meant to elicit sympathy—might prove the key to recasting a likable defendant as a habitual liar. If the trial team could show that she was deceptive about something such as commuting, they believed, they could ruin the positive "image" that would make any potential testimony resonate with jurors.

Ultimately, the defendant decided to testify. During a break after the first portion of her cross-examination, the prosecutor who was tasked with questioning her felt demoralized. A member of the jury appeared, in his view, to have "bought her story." He explained:

> I feel like if you said, "go tell the jury why she's a liar" I could do that in about thirty minutes, and I think I could convince all of them. The difficulty I'm having is they've created an insane story that is beautifully consistent with the evidence—at least as much as they could fit into it. She becomes a very difficult [defendant] to cross as opposed to just making an argument to the jury that she's a liar.

It would not be enough, in his view, to present the jury with evidence of discrete lies. The narrative integrity of the defendant's testimony would only be undermined if members of the jury felt they could not believe *anything* she said. The prosecutor asserted that he needed to "unmask" the defendant's untruthful character for all to see. Reveal negative character, annihilate credibility—this was the theory that implicitly guided various AUSAs as they crossed defendants and witnesses for the defense.

In other cases, the AUSAs faced the challenge of rehabilitating the character of their own witnesses who had committed crimes and told lies in the past. In such cases, prosecutors attempted to strike a delicate balance between distancing themselves from these witnesses—usually cooperating witnesses who previously engaged in the same illegal conduct as the defendant—and supporting their testimony.[10] Some worried that jurors might wonder if these cooperating witnesses were unindicted coconspirators who were just as culpable as the defendants in their cases or even more so. The imperfect solution to this problem hinged on character: prosecutors would use questions and language to show jurors that these witnesses were not habitual liars but rather thoughtful people who only lied in very specific circumstances (e.g., when engaging in criminal activity). Lying, the prosecutors wished to make clear, was something these witnesses could choose to do or not do. By cooperating, they had given evidence that they had chosen to tell the truth.

The complexity of this process was evident in one memorable meeting in which a prosecutor reflected on aspects of a cooperator's testimony that he believed jurors would view as evidence of his truthful character. He was particularly interested in the cooperating witness's responses to questions that spoke to lapses in judgment or memory. He reasoned that jurors would find this relatable, drawing particular attention to the witness's responses to several questions with "I don't recall" or "I don't know." "If he is a liar," the prosecutor offered, "why would he say he doesn't remember? He would totally fill in all kinds of details."

His colleagues agreed. It stood to reason that a pathological liar would not be able to control himself and would continue to lie—however small or irrelevant the point—if he stood to gain from it. "If you know you're making all this shit up," a colleague added, "just make up more—a little bit more of a lie."

Then the hypothetical jurors entered the meeting. The trial team proceeded to imagine details that the cooperator *could* have concocted to further incriminate the defendant. For example, the cooperator admitted to forgetting key details from the numerous, consensually-recorded phone conversations he had had with the defendant in which they discussed the crime in question. He could have embellished and invented these details. Instead, the cooperator told the jury that he could not remember specifics from the conversations. But this was a positive thing, according to the prosecutors: it gave evidence of good character, which was at least as important as what the witness actually had to say.

This was true not only of cooperating witnesses. Once, a prickly government official who agreed to testify for the prosecution was called "vindictive" by the defense. The prosecutors were confident that the characterization would not stick for the jury, given that the witness, despite her abrasive manner, had gone out of her way to express sympathy for the defendant.

"That this employee could at first come off as such an asshole and then as compassionate," a member of the trial team explained during a break, "makes you realize that people are complicated. Everybody's got their petty jealousies, everybody's got their confidants, everybody's got those things, and those things change all the time."

In this prosecutor's view, the employee's credibility was tied to lay outsiders' ability to "see themselves" in her by identifying with her idiosyncrasies. Once more, whatever the importance of the testimony itself, character—endorsed, impugned, unmasked—remained a central fixation of the AUSAs at all stages of the trial.

Credible Victims

There is a final "character" that must be discussed when considering the centrality of character judgment in the work of federal prosecutors: victims. Examining rape trials, anthropologists have drawn attention to the domination at work in legal processes. John Conley, William O'Barr, and Gregory Matoesian, for instance, suggest that features of the rape trial enable it to oppress a victim in very particular ways, as a victim must confront both her alleged rapist and an aggressive defense attorney. These and other scholars also highlight the way explicit and implicit references to a victim's past sexual history are used to discredit testimony and undermine character. They describe the "double bind" a sex crime victim confronts: showing a lack of emotion will suggest the victim is calculating and dishonest, while displaying an abundance of emotion will imply the victim is irrational and hysterical.[11] In the context of the William Kennedy Smith prosecution, for instance, Matoesian demonstrates how the defense attorney carefully deployed a strategy to impeach the victim's character by way of a "multiplex configuration of legal reasoning and linguistic hegemony."[12] Throughout his analysis, Matoesian underscores the calculating linguistic tactics of the lawyers, such as their "molecular strategies of identity negotiation" and their exploitation of "an array of intersecting discursive mechanisms."[13]

I witnessed this exact process as an observer of federal trials. In one case, for instance, a young female victim was variously characterized by the defense as too distant temporally from the crime to recall it accurately, too promiscuous to have not consented to a sexual encounter with the defendant, and too contemptuous of the truth—the defense showed she had once registered for an eighteen-plus website before she was eighteen years old!—to give a credible account of what had occurred. All of this was meant to overcome a mountain of damning and categorical evidence, including phone records, GPS data, and observations by witnesses who lived in the defendant's neighborhood. Her character was the only thread the defense could pull, and thus to keep the case from unraveling, the AUSAs worked to protect it, refuting each slanderous accusation.

But in this case, there was an additional problem: a staggering number of errors and details in the victim's personal account that contradicted things she had said previously. These were all sensible— she had, after all, been subjected to a violent crime without the ability to determine the exact time and place where everything occurred. Still, one could—as the prosecutor did—imagine jurors for whom these kinds of discrepancies mattered. At the end of one trial day, the lead prosecutor was unnerved—it was not clear that this was the kind of victim who could be narratively rehabilitated. "It's impossible to imagine how it could have gone worse," he said. "She was terrible. She completely derailed—gave stuff up that was a whole new story, different from her grand jury testimony and different from this, and then would just sit there."[14]

With the victim's character—and perhaps the entire case—on the line, the prosecutors came up with an unusual but ingenious plan: they would concede that *all* of the victim's testimony might have been fabricated but still assert that the plethora of other evidence and testimony proved their case beyond a reasonable doubt. In his closing argument, the prosecutor suggested that the jury engage in a "thought experiment" and consider that the victim had not testified. Would they not still conclude based on the very damning circumstantial evidence that the defendant was guilty? In this and other cases in which the character of the victim had been convincingly demolished, prosecutors typically added one last reminder: it is not the government that chooses victims, but the defendants. And they choose particular victims who seem variously naive, vulnerable, or credulous—the very traits, the AUSAs implied, that made them poor witnesses.

Competing Ideologies and Conflicts of Loyalty

What makes someone credible in the twenty-first-century United States? Though the prosecutors never asked this question directly, their fixation on the character of victims, defendants, witnesses, and jurors meant that they often reflected on potential markers of credibility. Two markers that came up repeatedly were religiosity and political affiliation—both forms of involvement in larger causes or collectivities that prosecutors worried might affect what people said or, in the case of jurors, *heard*, during a trial. Recall that this chapter opened with one AUSA's assumption that listening to a particular radio show meant it was likely that a prospective juror had particular views. This was enough to tag this person—a complete stranger—as a "bad juror." In other cases, it was where a person lived that mattered. Here, geography became shorthand for likely political affiliation and a constellation of specific attributes and perceptions that were imputed to the juror—including a belief that global warming was a hoax, that the government was too large and corrupt, that taxes should be abolished, that punishments should be harsh deterrents for criminals. In some cases, I learned from the prosecutors, you might want that kind of juror. In others, you would not. Prosecutors also worried that jurors might be swayed by political rhetoric they read in newspapers or on social media or heard discussed on television. In one case that involved the alleged mistreatment of undocumented immigrants by a federal law enforcement agent, even though the prosecutors leading the case had initially referred to it as a "straightforward" prosecution, the tenor of their discussions shifted in the wake of public controversy about migration at the southern border. Concerned that jurors might erroneously see immigration policy at the heart of the case, colleagues implored members of the trial team to remove lines like "this is not a case about building a wall."

Here, again, the jurors' imagined party affiliations informed the trial team's framing of its evidence. Yet the prosecutors disagreed on the extent to which information gleaned during voir dire shed light on jurors' political leanings. Noting the tenuous relationship between media preferences and likely attitudes toward their case, one prosecutor asked, facetiously, whether his colleagues would prefer a juror who said, "I watch Fox News, I read Breitbart," or another who said, "I watch MSNBC, I read *The Nation*." The answer, as their discussion showed, was not so clear. Though a juror who consumed stereotypically conservative news media might be critical of a law enforcement officer who attempted to harbor undocumented immigrants, the same juror might just as readily accept the officer's testimony out of respect or reverence for law enforcement in general. [15]

As with politics, I witnessed prosecutors reflect on the utility of religious beliefs. A not uncommon topic in jury selection was whether potential jurors' religions were a casual activity or a totalizing knowledge system that would preclude following legal instructions and casting judgment. One widely repeated anecdote among the attorneys in the office concerned a prospective juror who identified as a Jehovah's Witness. When asked if he could fairly and impartially serve as a juror in a criminal case, he matter-of-factly explained that he did not believe that *any* person should pass judgment on any other. This power, in his view, was reserved for God alone. Some AUSAs invoked this story to make the point that such an approach was possible among all jurors of intense faith—they were to be avoided. At the same time, some prosecutors voiced skepticism about the story's import and referenced their own research or personal experience to challenge what they perceived to be stereotypes.[16] In any case, however, the AUSAs would likely be wary of any juror who insisted on invoking religious texts and rigidly applying such doctrine to their deliberations and judgment.

Race and Socioeconomic Status as Evidence

The work of casting aspersions or otherwise denigrating the character of people whose professional credentials and lifestyles were similar to those of the prosecutors was different from doing so with people who were clearly different from the prosecutors. These latter people were predominantly poor defendants of color charged with gun and drug felonies. Prosecutors' commentaries on the different labor they devoted to discrediting or otherwise engaging in character attacks on such individuals, like the law enforcement–focused biases they sought out during voir dire, exposed a pronounced and racialized outlook that insinuated itself into every aspect of their work. Prosecutors appeared to find it more difficult to undermine the character of affluent professionals like themselves whom they imagined jurors would relate to.[17] In the white-collar cases I observed, for example, witnesses were predominantly white and did not have criminal records or any previous negative contact with law enforcement. Many had advanced degrees. Some worked as attorneys, and one was a former judge. The extensive narrative work prosecutors devoted to discrediting white-collar witnesses during cross-examination, on the assumption that jurors would view them favorably, spoke to their perception of such witnesses as more difficult to present as dishonest. This view was likely attributable to the ease with which the prosecutors related to such witnesses, a compatibility they expressed through the jurors they imagined.

Prosecutors commented on their orientation toward such witnesses in explicit terms. One, for example, noted the difficulty of conveying the importance of a prosecution for securities fraud to his adult daughter. He distinguished this case from "the kind of case you see on TV shows," which contain more "interesting stuff" for jurors. The difference, in his view, was the emotional impact of a case; no juror would "yawn and say ho hum" about a sex abuse case. Prosecutions of public officials, too, were believed to resonate with invented jurors. Yet some in the office worried that despite being "charlatans" in the business of "fleecing people," public officials facing prosecution would be among the most difficult defendants to depict as morally bankrupt. In contrast, prosecutors noted the visceral appeal of violent crime and drug cases. As one prosecutor commented, with such cases jurors could be told they would be taken "into a world you've never been to."

During a moot opening statement meeting in a different fraud prosecution, prosecutors noted that trying to villainize the defendant by pointing to his "greed and deceit" would be difficult. A prosecutor observed that the opening statement's reference to the defendant driving an expensive car might fall on deaf ears, since the defense attorney drove the same type of car. In other contexts, prosecutors made jokes that hinged on a similar perception of the consonance between witnesses' and jurors' life experiences. In a public corruption case, for example, prosecutors drew laughs when they pointed out that the phone number of an adult witness recorded in a wiretap transcript belonged to a cell phone family plan paid for by his mother.

What the cases described in this chapter have in common is their demonstration of the centrality of character judgment to prosecutors' case preparation. And this is not surprising: behind the evidence rules' limitations on explicit reliance on character propensity evidence is recognition of the prevalence of such judgment. The matter of framing some witnesses as having a tendency to lie and others as being motivated to lie only on discrete occasions, however, is not stipulated by any rule or doctrine. For the prosecutors I observed, it was a collaborative and narrative task that they approached differently depending on the witness in question. Prosecutors with limited trial experience and little awareness of the characteristics of actual jurors in the district could only draw on their local knowledge and experience to imagine how ordinary people, in all of their subjectivity, might assess the credibility of those who supplied evidence in their cases. Ultimately, though, the scrutiny of aspects of a defendant's character might be, thanks to the rules of evidence, formally off-limits for the AUSAs. Discerning and recasting the character of witnesses and victims was, I discovered, a central part of the work of federal prosecution.

6

Judicial Discretion beyond Truth

The natural home of argument, reasoning, and justification
is not in the individual autonomous mind but in palpable
social interactions, whether face-to-face or in more medi-
ated forms—for even doctrinal texts imply an addressee.
—Webb Keane, *Ethical Life*

Once, on the final day of a trial, I asked an AUSA what it felt like to
await a jury verdict. He told me to watch a clip from the end of the 1998
movie *The Truman Show*. Here, the protagonist, Truman, discovers that
his entire life has been surreptitiously recorded and broadcast to the
world as a reality TV show. After learning the truth, he attempts to leave
his false world by sailing across an artificial ocean and exiting the set.
The public within the movie is completely absorbed by the climax of
Truman's story, as we see people around the world greet his successful
escape with cheers, screams, tears, and applause. With Truman's escape,
the show is finally over. The movie then cuts to two security guards
hunched over their own small TV. The screen that had seconds ago been
all-consuming is now blank. One guard turns to the other and asks what
else is on.

"That's us," the AUSA told me, referencing the movie. "What's next?"
The swiftness of the transition from total sensory focus to the search
for something else—this was this prosecutor's experience of the trial,
which shifted almost imperceptibly from an all-encompassing drama
to . . . nothing. Like the security guards, he looked for the next diversion,
lingering at the office to chat with colleagues, a researcher, anyone to dis-
tract from the tedium of waiting for the brief absorption of the verdict.

My own experience of the all-consuming universe of federal prosecution came when I was invited to closely follow a jury trial from start
to finish. It was a strange one. Because the defendants in this case were
charged with assault, and not homicide, the judge believed it would be

unfairly prejudicial to tell the jury that one of the victims was in fact dead. The judge therefore ruled, before trial, that the lawyers were *prohibited from mentioning the victim's death at any point* during the proceedings. To maintain the supposed integrity of the trial, the lawyers were to act as if the victim was simply unreachable, inaccessible, and uncontactable. This proved to be a challenge for the AUSAs involved, who had to navigate a judge-made legal fiction with which they vehemently disagreed.

This, as well as other trials I would come to observe wholly or in part, demonstrated how judges, too, rely on their own imagined jurors to make and justify decisions. Rather than overtly express skepticism about the government's case, the judge invoked jurors and what they would or would not find natural and self-evident.[1] In this manner, this judge—like the AUSAs—found the means for legitimating a potentially unpopular and even unethical decision by appealing to the views of laypeople who—it goes without saying—had not been consulted.

In theory, American judges serve as the neutral arbiters of jury trials. In the district that was the focus of this study, judges often emphasized the nonadversarial nature of their role by comparing themselves to umpires, traffic officers, and even, as one put it, facilitators of "laboratory conditions" within the courtroom. Some made a point of cautioning jurors against scrutinizing their demeanor during trial. One judge, for example, candidly explained that while he did not think he displayed facial expressions as witnesses testified, jurors should disregard any potential reactions—he did not want them to think to themselves, "Oh, the *judge* doesn't believe this witness!" Legal scholars have noted the importance of this detached orientation to proceedings, which is an instrumental part of the rapport judges establish with lay decision makers from voir dire through the end of trial.[2]

Of course, some AUSAs believed judges were not so cautious about making their opinions of testimony—or an entire case—known to jurors.[3] This has been noted by other empirical legal researchers, such as Susan Philips, whose ethnographic research in Tucson, Arizona, shows that even trial court judges who embrace an ideology of "impartiality" leave their imprint on proceedings with distinct normative views of due process, courtroom control, and citizenship.[4] Judges might also impact the trial, some prosecutors believe, through their interactions with lawyers in the courtroom. Instances of open disagreement, I was told, were to be avoided. "It might seem like the judge is reprimanding your case," one prosecutor said, "so you have to be aware of how it's being perceived by jurors all the time." The same prosecutor cautioned a colleague not to undermine the judge's courtroom control by trying to correct what they viewed as erroneous rulings—the judge could "snap" in front of the jury.[5] And who would the jury blame?

In this particular trial, these considerations of what jurors might think in hypothetical situations were explicitly invoked by both prosecutors and the judge, shaping the context within which the various legal actors involved coproduced the legal process. The distinctive shape of the trial, including the sequence and parameters of its unfolding, reflected decisions that were made and justified, as usual, by imagining the reactions, evaluations, biases, and interpretive shortcomings of the public. What is striking is that in this case, make-believe jurors were called upon by the judge to obscure the facts and create a make-believe reality: the jurors, who had been summoned to pronounce on whether the defendants had committed assault, were not permitted to know that the victim had died.

Unindicted Homicide

To the judge, there was no other way to proceed. There was no homicide charge, so there could be victims but no *homicide victims*. The judge framed the decision as following obviously from Federal Rule of Evidence 403—the risk was too great that evidence of the victim's death would unfairly prejudice jurors against the defendants, and this substantially outweighed whatever probative value it might have for the case. This conclusion, of course, required imagining how jurors would actually react to this fact, and in this particular instance, only the judge's imagination mattered: it was simply common sense to the judge that the public was incapable of adjudicating this particular case if they learned what had actually happened. In a sense, the judge believed, jurors had to determine the truth but could not handle it.

The limiting instruction delivered instead of decreed by the judge—that the victim was simply inaccessible—left a number of questions unanswered. Where was the victim? Why couldn't federal prosecutors bring the victim to court? Where were the victim's medical records? How could a victim with such severe injuries ever fully recover? The judge was satisfied that the impartiality of the jury—a hypothetical one—would be maintained with the omission of the victim's death, largely overlooking or ignoring what to my mind seemed like obvious questions that would nag at jurors. But my imagined jurors, who would have perhaps justified a different approach, were irrelevant here.

Unsurprisingly, the ruling presented a narrative challenge for the trial team. For one thing, it required that another victim of the defendants testify *as if* the dead victim were still alive. What if the living victim violated the instruction? One AUSA described the situation as like walking through a minefield, since each direct examination question would have to be meticulously worded to not elicit a response from a traumatized witness that might unravel the artificial reality established within the courtroom and—could it seriously happen?—lead to a mistrial. The surreal character of this particular case was heightened by the allowance of the truth into discussions at sidebar, as the judge permitted the lawyers to freely discuss the date and circumstances of the one victim's death, as well as pieces of evidence that required additional redactions. When the jury reentered the courtroom, however, this was all made taboo again, and the trial proceeded with its core fiction.

Would it hold? Could it hold? One day, a defense attorney noticed a male juror eating lunch with a woman who regularly attended the trial as a spectator—and who was therefore privy to numerous discussions of the circumstances of the dead victim's absence. This revelation prompted panic among the judge and lawyers. How did the juror know this woman? And who was the person observing the trial? A journalist? A family member? Since the victim's death had been a topic of discussion in open court, after the jury had been dismissed, how could the trial proceed if a member of the public had conveyed this knowledge to the jury. The spectator, it turned out, was *the juror's spouse*. This had not been imagined by anyone. When questioned by the judge, the man explained that he and his wife never discussed the case, which they understood to be a violation of the rules. He was permitted to return to the jury box.

It did not matter. During the surviving victim's direct examination, an AUSA did the unthinkable, accidentally piercing the curtain between the trial's two realities. "You testified yesterday," the prosecutor began, "that when [the victim] was alive, you tried to . . ." A defense attorney later said he could see the jurors' eyes widen in shock as the prosecutor spoke. The prosecutor's use of the phrase "when [the victim] was alive," he argued, clearly suggested to jurors that the victim was *not* alive any longer. The defense further argued that no juror in the world would fail to connect an unexplained death to the actions of a defendant already on trial for grievously harming that victim. The AUSAs cited appellate cases suggesting that jurors could be urged to disregard precluded evidence they mistakenly heard in the courtroom. The bell—the metaphor went—could not be unrung, but perhaps its sound could be muffled. This prosecutor invoked an imagined jury that could be trusted to direct its attention away from the problematic words. The jury he imagined differed markedly from the one the judge imagined—and only the latter jury mattered. The defense moved for a mistrial.

The judge's assessment of the mistrial motion put jurors' imagined perspectives front and center. The judge argued that there was only one way for a juror to have interpreted the prosecutor's words: the victim was dead, killed by the defendants. It defied imagination and logic, the judge said, to think the jurors were capable of avoiding the obvious conclusion that the victim had been murdered. This conception of common sense hinged on the particular narrative formulation of the victim's life that the judge had fashioned in a pretrial ruling. Though the temporal parameters of this narrative erased the fact of the victim's death, it assumed a linear form and coherence of its own, even if it terminated in the person's mysterious unreachability. To interrupt this story with a death that was unexplained by the evidence would destroy its integrity. Another issue—whether the jury might feel like the judge and lawyers lied to them or deceived them—was never considered.

It was a mistrial.

Stranger Than Fiction: The Reset

"It's like *Groundhog Day!*" the judge announced at the start of the retrial. "Every day we start it again, we learn nothing. And start it again." The judge was not the only one to invoke the 1993 film in which Bill Murray is forced to repeat the same day over and over again. Others referred to it as well in witness preparation meetings, perhaps as a way to alleviate the tension surrounding the proceedings. During informal office conversations, the retrial was called the "reset."

It was immediately clear that the prosecution's strategy for the reset would be very different. Retrials presented the prosecutors with an unusual opportunity to reflect aloud on the uncertainty and flexibility of their work. In addition to being able to draw on the imagined impressions of past jurors during new prosecutions, they could revise presentations—and even selections—of evidence. One AUSA in the office once animatedly described a past case that resulted in two hung juries and three trials overall. In the lead-up to each trial, he eliminated and substituted witnesses based on his perception that previous jurors had found them untrustworthy or irritating. Likening trial preparation to directing a play, others emphasized the importance of looking hard at one's evidence and considering whether the case was stronger without certain pieces of it.

In addition to keying their preparation to the imagined perspectives of former and future jurors, the AUSAs for the reset oriented their strategy around the narrative constraints the judge had imposed on the jury's behalf. In the first trial, for example, an expert who had examined the victim before their death had testified that it was the worst case they had ever seen. The judge insisted that this type of claim was excessively prejudicial and should not be repeated. When the judge saw that this same witness was visibly distressed during the second trial, the judge commented, in an unrecorded aside, that crying would be interpreted as histrionics. Displays of unrestrained emotion, the judge made clear, were unprofessional and dangerous to the trial. On the record, the judge said that when people who had contact with the deceased victim were questioned, they should be instructed to rein in their feelings to avoid the theatrics of the last time around.

To the AUSAs trying this case, this instruction put the government in the difficult position of needing to modify affective dimensions of testimony by people who had seen deeply upsetting things. A prosecutor explained that these were individuals who dealt with human beings—not office supplies—for a living. Shows of emotion, this prosecutor argued, would convey earnestness to the laypeople evaluating the testimony.

But the jurors the judge imagined had a different view of tears, weeping, and emotion. In keeping with the intuitions of these jurors, the judge required that these witnesses refrain from characterizing the victims' conditions in comparative terms by commenting, for example, that the case before them was the worst they had ever seen, or that the victims had been harmed more than other victims they had seen. "We don't need the optics," the judge said.

A prosecutor urged the judge to reconsider this position. How was a professional witness's comparison of two victims' appearances different from the comparison of, say, two patients' lab results? It was different, the judge responded the next day, because it was subjective: testimony that the victim was the *most badly injured victim* was different from testimony that an X-ray image of a person's arm depicted the greatest number of fractures, which could be objectively quantified. The latter was a kind of comparison that was beyond dispute, the logic went. The former? This was unreliable and colored by factors that were difficult, if not impossible, to identify.

In an effort to limit the prejudicial interpretation that the judge had imputed to jurors, another instruction was given: the answer that compared the victim to other victims would be struck and was to be disregarded. The judge further instructed the actual jury that the witness could not make any conclusions or determinations of whether the victim was assaulted, since this was the ultimate legal issue.

During a later meeting with supervisors, one of the AUSAs expressed frustration over the judge's demand that witnesses change their demeanors in the name of fictitious jurors. If someone with direct contact with the victims of the case sat stoically, he contended, such testimony would ring hollow to jurors. It was the witness's affect and expressive language that made the testimony seem authentic. By placing constraints on the prosecutors' preparation of their witnesses—and on witnesses' language—the judge would influence actual jurors' interpretations of their testimony in the name of imaginary ones.

At other points during the trial, the judge worried aloud that the prosecutors might unduly shape jurors' factual interpretations. When a prosecutor commented that a defense witness appeared confused after she asked a question, for example, the judge chastised the prosecutor in front of the jury. The judge then asked the jury to disregard the prosecutor's characterization of the witness as looking perplexed—adding that members of the jury could decide this for themselves. The judge's encouragement of jurors to make their own credibility assessments based on a witness's demeanor seemed appropriate to the trial team. But the judge's tone and apparent frustration with the prosecutors worried them, as they imagined how this was perceived by the jury.

As with the first trial, the reset had its close calls. When a prosecutor mentioned a date and inadvertently omitted the deceased victim from a description of the situation, the judge noted the mistake in a sidebar commentary. The judge reminded those present that the jury would likely speculate on the fate of the victim based on aggregated evidence. *We* know the whole story, the judge said, but the jurors should not. Inevitably, the judge continued, they would begin linking things up by drawing on hints, clues, and other subtle ways that the prosecutors might reveal the victim's death. The judge observed that the jurors had common sense: give them enough and they would infer that the victim was not just deceased but killed. There was only so much fiction, the judge offered, that they could push down this jury's throat.

Reinterpreting Jurors

In the end, the jury found the defendants guilty of assault. The judge's control of the trial, however, did not end with the defendants' conviction. The judge was concerned that the potential prejudice against the defendants would carry over to sentencing, and openly condemned the punishment sought by the government as too severe. Though the judge said that the jury's findings would not be ignored, the sentence to be imposed would be grounded in the judge's sense of the defendants' character. These were the same intuitions that oriented the judge's efforts to curate the evidence that jurors saw at trial. The verdict that the jury in fact rendered was largely absent from the judge's reflections during the sentencing proceedings.

The judge called the jury's verdict sheet "very naked" and filled in supposed narrative gaps with an original narrative that suggested deep ambivalence about the extent of the defendants' culpability. The judge expressed an unwillingness to accept the government's story about what caused the victims' injuries. With respect to the injuries of the victim who had later died, in particular, the judge's dissatisfaction was explicit. Actual jurors—now gone from the courtroom—were quickly replaced by the judge with like-minded imaginary ones. When I come upon these kinds of allegations, the judge shared, I have a case where I can't be sure that a jury of their peers, in fact, found this. It was as if by directing attention to evidence jurors were *not* shown—for example, evidence of the victim's demise—the judge could interpret the jury's silence on the matter as exculpatory.

The judge imposed sentences that were later deemed excessively lenient by the court of appeal. The appellate court's ruling cited the judge's own expressions of empathy and compassion for one of the defendants, linking possible misdeeds to the general human propensity to make mistakes. And the court did not hold back: it was inappropriate for a judge to voice sympathy for a defendant found guilty of assaulting others. What exactly, the court challenged, had this person done to deserve sympathy? Continuing, the court of appeal turned to particular comments from the sentencing hearing. These, the court argued, revealed a level of skepticism on the part of the judge that was difficult to reconcile with the jury's verdict. First, the court cited and questioned the judge's use of a sports analogy to ridicule the lengthy prison sentence that prosecutors had requested for the defendants. The judge had been incredulous, commenting that the prosecution was not a game: "This is not how many touchdowns do we win by!" Though the court of appeal acknowledged that the judge was not required to agree with the sentences proposed by the government, it viewed the judge's comparison of the prosecutors' arguments to football as making a mockery of the victims' suffering. The court of appeal likewise criticized the judge's comment that the defendants had not committed real federal offenses because "society as a whole was not harmed" by them.

The opinion ended with scrutiny of the judge's references to the defendants' courtroom behavior and physical appearance. The district court judge had noted in particular that unlike defendants who come to court sloppily dressed or late, these defendants were courteous and punctual and appeared to get along with their attorneys. This conduct, the judge said, was inconsistent with the monstrous things the government claimed they had done to their victims. The court of appeal ended its opinion by returning to the verdict. Regardless of the judge's efforts to re-narrate the case, the court emphasized that it was an *actual jury* that returned a guilty verdict. Imagined jurors might legitimate decisions—even unthinkable ones—but they could not overrule the will of an actual jury.

Every trial is to some extent its own *Truman Show*, though it is not the AUSAs but the actual jurors whose world—the courtroom—is shaped by dimly understood forces beyond their control. The odd case described in this chapter highlights the remarkably creative power of judges, who, like the federal prosecutors in this book, appeal to the perspectives of their own hypothetical laypeople to allow certain actions and utterances and disallow others. What we discover is that in this regard a legal process that is meant to get to the truth of the matter often stands upon various fictions—some of which can only be justified by appealing to the anticipated views of fictional jurors. That the Federal Rules of Evidence are oriented around such inferential leaps is an inbuilt part of an adversarial system designed for actual—though ultimately unknowable—laypeople. And because cases are ultimately settled by groups rather than individuals, the collective negotiation and refiguration of such jurors emerged (whether in a courtroom or a prosecutor's office) as a vital context for sharing, challenging, or reconciling discordant opinions.

Importantly, this case highlights the untenability of a criminal legal system that nearly sacralizes the jury—invoking it constantly—while reducing the number of jury trials to a mere fraction. Here, it was only the deliberation and decision-making of a real jury that permitted a court of appeal to condemn behaviors and statements that seemed questionable at best. This was a stark reminder that the value of the American jury hinges on its ability to introduce the actual, commonsense perspectives of the public into the legal process. That ability is not a given: it is within our control to amplify or diminish the real impact of laypeople in the American legal system.

Conclusion

The impact of the jury on the popular imagination remains
critical, and since many state and national cases operate in
the shadow of a potential jury trial, their role in the United
States and elsewhere remains, like the miner's canary or an
indicator species, an important sign of the culture of law as
a whole.
—Lawrence Rosen, *Law as Culture: An Invitation*

Though numerous conversations with prosecutors in the course of my
fieldwork have stayed with me, there is one that is particularly vivid.
A senior prosecutor in the office described being asked in a civics
class which amendment within the Bill of Rights she thought was the
most important. She recalled that her peers said the First Amendment
because it protected their religious beliefs. She thought this was child-
ish. Her own response, which she recounted with pride, was the Sixth
Amendment and its right to a trial by jury. When asked by her teacher
to explain this unusual answer, she remembered saying that without the
right to a jury trial, no *other* right could be protected.

Her feelings about the importance of juries had not changed in the
intervening years. "Jurors react here," she said to me, placing her hand
on her chest, "and on the way up, it hits the brain"—her hand moved
to her face—"and they come up with an answer." What she meant by
this, and later elaborated, is that laypeople rely on instincts before rationalizations, on common sense before expertise. And it was this kind of
decision-making that made their judgment meaningful and impactful.

A significant feature of federal prosecutors' work is its orientation
toward the figure of the juror. As I discovered in the US attorney's office,
this orientation helps them to develop their cases, navigate questions
of credibility and character, manage potentially difficult collaborations,
and reflect on the ethics of prosecution. All of this exemplifies what legal

scholar Robert Burns has referred to as the "human dimension of legal questions that can be lost in piles of briefs and records."[1] The presence of imagined jurors, in its own limited way, has a democratizing effect on prosecutions, forcing these representatives of the government to engage to some extent with alternative formulations of justice. When prosecutors imagine and express intuitions that might be shared by the public, they consider "ordinary moral and commonsense reasoning," and this, I think, shapes the relatively wide discretion afforded to them.[2]

This is true not just for line attorneys in the criminal division. In the civil context, too, legal scholars have noted that what I have called "imagined," hypothetical," or "make-believe" jurors inform attorneys' assessments of likely damage awards during settlement negotiations.[3] John Guinther and Bettyruth Walter argue, for example, that "juries have a function even when they aren't functioning. That is, decisions are regularly made about the course a case will take based on the participants' beliefs of what would *likely* happen if the case were tried by a jury."[4] It is thus clear, in the run of cases, that the influence of jurors exceeds their physical presence in courtrooms.[5]

But let me be very clear: imagined jurors are *no* substitute for the people summoned to court to participate in trials. In fact, the power of hypothetical jurors—and it is in most cases a limited power—is derived entirely from the small but real chance that a case might actually lead to a jury trial. Though it is impossible to prove, I believe that the greater that chance is, the more that imagined jurors will figure not just as avatars of a prosecutor's own desires and biases, but as part of a process of seeing a case from the perspective of a diverse American public. Beyond wanting more jury trials for their own sake (though this is a good reason), we should recognize that their greater frequency would likely strengthen the influence of the hypothetical jurors who I have shown empirically are present in all phases of prosecutorial work.

A further and related caveat: just because federal prosecutors talk extensively and regularly about their imagined jurors does not mean that these jurors represent the public. Often, as we have seen, stereotyped or skewed conceptions of laypeople are deployed and reinforced for the purpose of legitimating a particular prosecutor's view of things. Here, the jury is instrumentalized in order to direct case preparation in ways that conform merely to how a prosecutor thinks things should be done.

It is therefore critical to acknowledge the potential for unjust decision-making practices to flow from references to imagined jurors, while affirming the value of a functional and representative lay participation system to lawyers' work.

In assessing whether justice is served by the consideration of lay perspectives, several factors are worth considering. First, it is possible that the invocation of hypothetical jurors among judges, prosecutors, and units within prosecutors' offices reflects different levels of experience with developing and trying cases. Those with less trial experience, for example, may find lay decision makers less relevant to their day-to-day work, as the jury remains, truly, a distant abstraction. And this matters, as imagined jurors might make the difference in whether the office chooses to prosecute a case. For example, an AUSA described declining a case involving the unauthorized importation of medical equipment because of who she imagined would be in the jury box. It was not hard to imagine a prosecutor in a different US attorney's office—with a different local public—who would have been presented with the same evidence and opted to prosecute.

Second, as prosecutors look for defendants that "fit the part" for their imagined jurors, it is possible there are incentives to choose cases with defendants who seem superficially more threatening (or *less* sympathetic)—something that might lead to the disproportionate prosecution of those who already have criminal records. Finally, legal scholars and practitioners in the United States have long advanced arguments about the potential for jury verdicts to be "unpredictable and arbitrary, susceptible to being moved by factors which do not have to do with the evidence."[6] Debates about jurors' right to be informed about their power to disregard—or "nullify"—the law point to a similar source of ambivalence about discretionary judgment with limited oversight.[7]

Ethnographic Contributions to the Study of Prosecutorial Ethics

In offering an ethnographic account of federal prosecutors and their shared imagining of jurors, this book illuminates some of the less tangible effects of a jury system in decline. It relocates the jury and its influence by examining the identities and knowledge that prosecutors ascribe to laypeople as they engage in nearly every aspect of their work.

Rather than proving or disproving a particular theory of lay participation in the legal system, ethnographic research furnishes insight into the interpretive worlds of legal actors on a day-to-day basis. In this way, it refines the very analytic terms and assumptions that guide one's research. It also provides insight into how legal reforms—which have their own objectives—are actually incorporated into the legal system. This study has shown, for instance, how antidiscrimination law actively affects the way prosecutors think and speak about race. Ultimately, it is only by shedding empirical light on prosecutorial work—and the centrality of the jury in that work—that it becomes possible to understand, and attempt to improve, a system in which real and imagined laypeople contribute to a fairer legal process for all.

Attention to the social and collaborative means by which prosecutors exercise discretion builds on the work of anthropologists and sociolegal researchers in adjacent fields. Much attention to legal language to date has focused on case outcomes, including verdicts and judicial opinions, perhaps due in part to what Clifford Geertz has described as a "'how-to' bias" among scholars that treats the effects of legal practice as constitutive of the law more generally.[8] Such analyses of legal language, which typically adopt backward-looking reasoning from already settled ends, can conceal the inherently contingent, collaborative, and improvisational character of legal practice.[9] More recent interdisciplinary studies of legal narratives, however, capture their dynamic character, shaped by rules and principles that legal actors deploy differently.[10] For anthropologists and sociolegal scholars, these insights confirm that legal practice is interactive and creative.[11] Through this lens, even statements made in court can be appreciated for their collaborative nature.

To this end, ethnographic studies of lawyers' speech have shed light on how everything from case theories and grand jury presentations to opening statements and judicial opinions are part of a process of co-narration through which multiple or contested accounts are "fused."[12] In the context of studying the Franklin County District Court in Massachusetts, for example, Barbara Yngvesson observes that clerks flexibly and reflexively distinguish cases of everyday "trouble" (e.g., children fighting) from those of "disorder" that prompt court intervention.[13] Her work shows too how imagined audiences are mobilized to shape legal meaning.[14] In one case she analyzes, a man was charged with threatening public safety by cut-

ting down a tree that might have injured a child as it fell. The clerk, however, rephrased the language of this grievance to reflect what he imagined
was the public's more pressing concern: residents must not destroy public
property.[15] This act of linguistic reframing was neither a natural nor an inevitable result of "applying" law or being guided by legal discourse. Rather,
it was the result of the legal hearing offering an "arena" in which distinct
interpretative standpoints could intersect.

Anthropologist Justin Richland's study of the "interpretive ambiguity" in Hopi disputes adds to this insight, showing that although cases
may construe Hopi traditional practices as precedential authority or
objectionable hearsay, the outcomes that flow from their adjudication
are in no way preordained.[16] In a similar vein, Richard Wilson's ethnographic work on international criminal tribunals underscores the
improvisational quality of legal history storytelling, as the evidentiary
practices of one tribunal do not dictate—and in fact could have little
bearing on—the findings of another.[17] Variation between international
justice institutions thus militates against a view of legal discourse as
rigid or hegemonic. In each case, lawyers' language, whether written or
spoken, is dynamic and contingent, subject to refashioning as both their
strategies and those of other legal actors shift.[18]

The case narratives that trial lawyers create, both in conversation and
in preparation for potential trials, are critical subjects of ethnographic
study in their own right. One prosecutor analogized his focus on jurors' perceptions of opening statements to his process of evaluating FBI
agents' case pitches early in an investigation. "It's almost like the script
is flipped," he explained.

I'm now the jury and the agent is trying to convince me it's something
worth doing, and the same process is taking place. I may not consciously
be thinking to myself, "What will a jury think of this," but what I *am*
saying to myself is "Is this the kind of thing we should be concerned
about?" When you put yourself in this position, you're put in the position
of thinking, "What kind of appeal is this going to have?"

The hypothetical juror thus created an opening for legal actors to view
and evaluate their cases with fresh eyes, as though they had switched
roles and power positions.

Prosecutors' engagement with the interpretive worlds of potential jurors cannot be explained only by their interest in winning convictions. Despite conveying certainty and confidence in the strength of their evidence in advance of grand jury presentations, and indeed even in the lead-up to FBI agents' "takedowns" of targets of investigations, prosecutors devoted an inordinate amount of time and energy to elaborating the perspectives of future jurors. AUSAs who had previously worked in state offices often commented on their luxury, in federal court, of having amassed an abundance of evidence, including wiretap transcripts, video recordings, and witnesses. What federal prosecutors' sustained focus on jurors suggests is that this imaginative labor functions in part as a flexible ethical resource—enabling prosecutors to conceptualize what it means to be a good prosecutor, in both senses.

The character of the legal technique exercised by federal prosecutors through their imagined jurors, in this respect, is distinguished by its flexibility and contingency. Building on the work of Marilyn Strathern and others, Annelise Riles has articulated a vision of legal technique as a practice that involves "skill," "art," "bricolage," and the "satisfaction of rehearsing," and that encompasses a "constellation of material and aesthetic features" rather than being "tethered" to a particular outcome.[19] This view of legal technique resonates with those of other sociolegal scholars. Donald Brenneis, writing on bureaucracy, describes this kind of technique as operating in a mode of "situational participation" in which analytic categories are fungible, continually negotiated, and made intelligible with reference to imagined audiences.[20] In the related context of an institutional review board, Laura Stark shows how the aesthetics of a document can affect practices of evaluation. In serving as both literal and figurative "records," documents, including meeting minutes, become creative instruments, enabling participants to modify their speech for both real and imagined audiences.[21]

Other discussions of legal technique have similarly embraced the multitude of possible outcomes it can facilitate.[22] Enlarging and reimagining our language of technique can help ethnographers capture the craft of real-time knowledge production. And approaching legal technique as a social practice can help us move away from its constraining formulation as a skeleton or vessel into which meanings are "filled."[23]

Another analogue to federal prosecutors' conceptual work can be found in ethnographic studies of category creation in other social settings. Ira Bashkow's research on the Orokaiva in Papua New Guinea, for example, revealed a similar technique of invoking hypothetical constructs of strangers to render judgment. For the Orokaiva, conceptions of foreigners were tied to ideas about abstracted qualities, activities, and objects understood as "detachable from persons."[24] Likewise, prosecutors conceived of justice with reference to characteristics they ascribed to the occupations of imagined citizens and the places and institutions they affiliated with. Though jurors—like foreigners for the Orokaiva—rarely appeared in person, they remained an abundant and generative foil for their creators, as they contributed to the identity formation of those who invoked them. Even the remote possibility that a juror's judgment might later intervene in a prosecution justified this exercise, as prosecutors considered multiple and sometimes competing perspectives on their work.

Ethnographic attention to prosecutors' everyday work illuminates their decisions to decline or pursue cases, adjust investigative approaches or strategies, develop opening statements, evaluate prospective jurors, and distinguish being professional from being overzealous in their orientations toward juries. Beyond its more theoretical contributions to the study of legal decision-making, ethnographic research brings into relief the necessity and, indeed, urgency of taking concrete steps to enhance the democratic character of juries in the United States today. The jury system offers a site in which the law is given moral meaning by prosecutors. Significantly, it offers a process whereby professional legal actors imagine laypeople as moral beings shaped by divergent interests, occupations, family arrangements, and beliefs about the effectiveness of the legal system.

Diversity and Equality within the Prosecutor's Office

The AUSAs perceived their own discretion to be limited by lay decision makers. This, I believe, underscores the power of their ideas about ordinary people. The question of *how* prosecutors created and gave meaning to such jurors could also be determinative of whether the interests of justice were undermined in particular contexts and cases. A key resource prosecutors draw on to develop and invoke their imagined audience is information generated from the actual people who report for jury service or figure in colleagues' reflections from previous trials. They also draw on their own local knowledge from "proxy" jurors who include nonlawyer friends, family, and other acquaintances. As this book has shown, these contacts were generative for prosecutors, as they introduced frames of interpretation and repertoires of experience that broadened their personal conceptions of justice. Where one prosecutor might believe testimony provided by one family member against another should be included in a case, for example, another might draw on the opinions of surveyed relatives and friends to share the contrary view that even admissible and probative evidence can cross ethical lines.

With prosecutors' reliance on contact with people they know, however, comes the possibility—and, indeed, likelihood—that they will fail to imagine or consider the views of individuals who are different from them. A prosecutor's office that consists mostly of white, male, and well-to-do attorneys in possession of undergraduate and law degrees from elite schools might struggle to consider the views of a diverse and unequal public. And when prosecutors impute ideas born of their own experience to the jurors they present to colleagues and supervisors, they may help limit the range of options and outcomes for their cases. If the lives and opinions of actual jurors inform imagined ones, the absence of actual jury trials will only lead to the distancing of professional lawyers from the lay decision makers central to our adversarial system's design.

An important consequence of the homogeneity of the AUSAs is the presence of a tacit professional language of privilege within the office—notwithstanding the presence of line attorneys of color, women, and some lawyers who expressed concern about significant school debt and other forms of financial precarity. Most supervisors in the office during the time I spent there were white and male. The ideal imagined jurors to emerge in the case discussions among prosecutors I witnessed resembled their creators. They were presumed to be financially autonomous enough to devote full attention to the directives and necessities of jury service, which could call upon them for weeks or months. They were presumed to watch the news, access social media, and form opinions about events in the world during their discretionary time. They were presumed to trust—or to *want* to trust—the law enforcement agents who might testify at trial. And their presumed distrust of cooperating witnesses was thought to stem from their skepticism and distrust of those with criminal records despite assurances of future truth-telling. Above all, jurors were imagined to abide by the law themselves. The disenfranchisement of convicted felons, in this respect, was a taken for granted feature of prosecutors' juror-creating landscape.[25]

The construction of jurors with whom prosecutors could relate may account for prosecutors' willingness to empathize with defendants and witnesses who seemed more relatable, too—by virtue, for example, of their socioeconomic status as professionals (such as doctors, lawyers, and elected officials) and their conformity with stereotypical tropes of the sympathetic victim (such as children, single parents, and others discussed in chapter 5). The dominance of the privileged hypothetical juror emerged explicitly as prosecutors worked collaboratively to discredit or damage the character of defendants, witnesses, and victims with whom they shared characteristics. In such cases, prosecutors deliberated at length and with meticulous attention to how best to depict relatable individuals as unworthy of belief and worthy of prosecution from the perspective of relatable imagined jurors. The audience for these protracted case discussions, in other words, consisted of hypothetical jurors who they believed shared experience and intuitions about justice with them.

A counterpoint to this approach could be seen in the work of prosecutors who assumed a distanced and generalized orientation toward jurors of color, those who faced financial or caretaking burdens, and those with past negative encounters with law enforcement. In these contexts, prosecutors readily, and self-consciously, articulated legalistic generalities about the jurors they imagined. They expressed concern, for example, that their excusal of a Black prospective juror might be viewed by the judge, or by their adversaries, as an act of exclusion toward *all* Black prospective jurors, and devoted little time to engaging with the multitude of personal characteristics that distinguished prospective jurors of color, as discussed in chapter 4. Likewise, prosecutors devoted little time or attention to probing the extent and nature of prospective jurors' financial burdens or encounters with law enforcement, as discussed in chapter 5. Prosecutors were generally satisfied by the conclusions they could draw from the bare knowledge that prospective jurors believed they had faced harassment, been subjected to unlawful searches, or been victims of unsolved crimes in the past. In this respect, prosecutors' labeling and attendant judgment of prospective jurors based on race and economic hardship became determinative of jurors' further questioning or empanelment. And in many cases prosecutors defended such assessments as evincing special sensitivity to their obligations under antidiscrimination law or sensitivity to the financial and caretaking obligations of those summoned to participate in jury service.

Given the number of cases that move through the prosecutor's office that involve defendants of color who are poor, prosecutors' disproportionate familiarity with privileged and racially homogeneous colleagues and contacts has implications for the way they apprehend justice in their cases. The homogeneity of a prosecutor's social milieu can thwart ethical deliberation about those who are most likely to face implicit (through discrimination) or tacit (through lack of material support) exclusion from the jury system. Everything about invented jurors' identities, frames of interpretation, and credibility was assigned to them by legal actors who contributed to the control of their communities without necessarily living within those communities.

The same critique may be lodged against judicial exercises of discretion, as elaborated in chapter 6. Judges who imagine jurors as tending to sympathize with defendants who appear to be repentant and deserving of mercy on the basis of their manners, appearance, and courtesy toward courtroom personnel may bring this kind of biased assessment to evidentiary rulings, sentences, or general dispositions toward particular defendants. Though some might applaud this for resulting in lenient treatment in some cases, others draw attention to the danger of unprincipled, and disparate, displays of favoritism in the criminal justice system.[26]

A related finding to emerge from this study is the value, if not necessity, of an egalitarian office environment. A prosecutor's ability to bring distinct notions of fairness to presentations and assessments of evidence was contingent on their ability to air disagreement freely and without professional consequence. To the extent that prosecutors expect to be able to bring contrary views of more ethical interpretations of evidence and applications of the law to collaborative decision-making contexts, the presence of intermediary supervisors with veto power could hamper such efforts. It was not uncommon during my research to learn that particular AUSAs chose to appeal—or encouraged peers to appeal—to more senior office leadership about case concerns, only to be disparaged for violating subordinate chains of communication and command. This not only bred ill will among prosecutors who perceived certain colleagues to receive preferential treatment, or a more collegial relationship with "the boss," but could also lead to the resentment of supervisors who were perceived to be unqualified or unsuited, in either experience or temperament, for their roles.

The average line attorney in the US attorney's office I studied was positioned under at least two supervising attorneys below the highest level of office leadership. Still, imagined jurors could facilitate open communication and mutual respect. Invocations of such jurors allowed for the impromptu and informal scrutiny of their work while, on a more practical level, offering a means of constructively and nonconfrontationally pressing colleagues on their views.

The influence of imagined jurors is also vulnerable to the critique that notwithstanding office hierarchies, prosecutors ought to take personal responsibility for their opinions no matter how unpopular or divisive. This includes decisions that contravene those of one's supervisor—which is a significant, if challenging, part of the job. It is arguably the greatest test of a prosecutor's character to let a decision of conscience compel a case decision, or outcome, that one perceives as just—regardless of the personal or professional repercussions.[27]

Reimagining the Jury System

The potential that imagined jurors have to serve as an ethical resource, a means of speaking about extralegal justice, and an impetus for more reflexive law enforcement work is ultimately contingent on the interventions of actual laypeople in the legal system.[28] Although jury participation in federal prosecutions today is largely a product of the machinations of lawyers, the importance of the jury trial to prosecutors' roles should not be understated—prosecutors with trial experience often imagined jurors with reference to the people they encountered in court.

Though trials by jury will not be feasible in every federal case, prosecutors' willingness and, indeed, ability to imagine jurors as bringing unpredictable and unfamiliar perspectives to the legal system necessitate the participation of a diversely constituted public.[29] It is thus critical to acknowledge the ways in which the contemporary American jury continues to fall short of its imagined ideal as an audience able to offer an external standard of moral judgment, akin, perhaps, to Adam Smith's "impartial spectator."[30] Here, we must ask what can be done to make jury participation more accessible.

One obvious impediment to jury participation, discussed in chapter 4, is the financial difficulty it can pose to citizens who cannot afford to lose income. Eligible jurors who face financial hardship may be as reluctant to participate in jury selection. At the same time, defendants may be unwilling to risk the lengthier sentence that would likely follow from a guilty verdict in a jury trial. The result is fewer jury trials, or jury trials with juries that consist disproportionately of people with the material means to participate.

Today, compensation for empaneled jurors in state court varies widely. According to data gathered by the National Center for State Courts, some jurisdictions refrain from compensating jurors for their first day of service, while others deny compensation for the first several days of service.[31] Still other states offer token compensation as jurors begin their service.[32] More than anything, failure to support the material needs of citizens for the duration of jury service conveys the impression that the legal system does not value or prioritize the vital function that jurors play in it. It also reflects a doctrinal blindness and practical indifference to the impact that disparate juror compensation has on judges' and litigants' ability to empanel representative juries. Increasing juror pay would be a promising first step toward more broadly and uniformly recognizing the value of jurors' labor. It would also affirm the inextricable connection between people's material well-being and capacity to contribute to a civic institution that demands a significant investment of time and intellectual energy.

Lost income is not the only burden imposed by jury service. Many prospective jurors—most of them women—face the challenge of trying to reconcile their obligations as jurors with their obligations as primary caregivers for others.[33] In many parts of the country, women fought vigorously to participate as jurors and were flatly rebuffed for nearly sixty years, after gaining the right to vote.[34] Today, many states offer an explicit exemption for those caring for children or the elderly.[35] There is little uniformity, however, in the way that states approach this exemption. A minority of states explicitly limit the exemption to those with childcare responsibilities.[36] Others have a designated exemption for breastfeeding mothers,[37] and still others offer an exemption so broad that it could theoretically excuse all mothers from jury service.[38] The inherent inconsistency that arises from judges' exercising discretion in evaluating—and ultimately granting—caretaking dismissals may lead parents to avoid reporting to court altogether, out of concern they will not have recourse if their concerns are dismissed and excusal denied.[39]

This must change. The socioeconomic, gender, and racial diversity of American juries can be enhanced by facilities and services that offer caregiving support to dependents. Given the gendered and racialized dimensions of employment and care, universal reforms that tackle sources of juror hardship, such as those discussed in chapter 4, would help build juries whose diversity reflects that of the country. Further, lawyers are right to think that jurors will be distracted from trials by concerns about their jobs and the safety of their dependents. This type of reform would move us closer to a paradigm of juror support that not only acknowledges but embraces prospective jurors as whole individuals—individuals with obligations and constraints, individuals whose personal and professional responsibilities do not disqualify them from fulfilling an essential civic duty.

Empirical research has shown, and continues to show, the persistence of race-based exclusion in the jury selection process.[40] This has led some legal scholars and practitioners to accept that the principle of race neutrality, under *Batson*, is impracticable, as race is an inescapable feature of legal strategy in the US criminal justice system.[41] Critics of the *Batson* framework have highlighted its limited capacity to identify and deter prosecutors who are of a mind to discriminate.[42] Explanations for the persistence of race-based exclusion have focused on the ease with which prosecutors motivated by racial animus can use the cover afforded by peremptory strikes to engage in discriminatory voir dire practices owing to limited guidance on how to draw the line between "neutral" and pretextual rationales for excusing jurors if an attorney's reasoning appears factually accurate and consistently applied to others in a jury pool.[43] These long-standing deficiencies in the antidiscrimination law governing jury selection raise the question of whether reform efforts might be better served by targeting the point at which many jurors are excluded from service, based on past contact with law enforcement and other racially patterned experiences, as discussed in chapter 5, during the cause challenge phase of jury selection proceedings.

Addressing jury exclusion in this way would not necessarily require assumptions about one's propensity to engage in prejudicial decision-making. This would be a benefit of such a reform, since explicit expressions of racial animus are not solely responsible for systemically racist legal processes and outcomes.[44] Just as gender norms are formulated in the context of patriarchally minded rape prosecutions, race is constructed in the jury selection process via a white-centric "moral interpretive order" that judges and lawyers tacitly reinforce.[45]

The aim of highlighting these empirically grounded priorities for reform is to enhance the inclusivity of the jury system for all people eligible to serve as jurors, which not only could impart greater legitimacy to the legal system through the inclusion of historically suppressed voices but could also lead to fairer case outcomes for defendants.[46] Social scientists have highlighted a number of the jury system's other virtues, including the higher likelihood that people will vote if they have previously served as jurors.[47] Focusing on civil trials in particular, empirical studies have drawn attention to the favorable impressions of the fairness of the legal system generated by jury participation.[48] Other studies have highlighted the extent to which the jury confers legitimacy on the legal system and enhances its democratic character by allowing ordinary people to render judgment, contribute to a fact-finding body, and reap the benefits of an educational resource.[49] Some of the jury system's perceived legitimacy may even stem from the idea that its decision making processes are inherently unknowable—a "black box"—in nature.[50]

But we cannot take this legitimacy for granted. Across the Atlantic, Norway offers a cautionary tale of what can happen when people lose confidence in a jury system that exalts the judgment of nonlawyers.[51] After years of scholarly debate and anticipation, Norwegian politicians reached an agreement in 2017 to replace the all-layperson juries that had hitherto participated in appellate trials with a mix of lay jurors and professional judges.[52] This reform reflected distrust in the all-layperson, Anglo-American jury and the triumph of public and political belief in the capacity of laypeople and professionals to collaborate as equals. In the jury's place, Norway chose to institute a "mixed court" system in which lay and professional judges jointly deliberated about the guilt and sentences of criminal defendants.

The demise of Norway's all layperson jury system was not sudden. In fact, it resulted from a century of reflection about how laypeople ought to participate in the legal system and about whether their interventions were even necessary. The all-layperson juries in Norway resembled those in the United States. Judges in Norway instructed jurors not to conduct independent research or discuss their cases in advance of formal deliberations, and verdicts were rendered anonymously, though without a unanimity requirement.[53] A finding of guilt required that seven of the ten jurors respond affirmatively to the yes-or-no questions outlined for them on a verdict form.[54] If the panel of professional judges accepted their verdict, two randomly selected male and two female jurors (including the foreperson) joined them to determine the defendant's punishment.[55]

As in the United States, prosecutors in Norway approached their cases differently depending on whether they thought a juror or a professional judge would assess the evidence. When prosecutors prepared to face all-layperson juries, they adapted their word choice and presentations of evidence to the varied expertise and experiences of ordinary citizens. Prosecutors who prepared their cases for professional judges, in contrast, did not invent a hypothetical lay audience and accepted that professional judges were likely to have a significant influence on the lay judges with whom they deliberated.

The American and Norwegian legal systems differ in significant respects that underscore the importance of autonomous and representative lay decision makers in the United States in particular. High social inequality and sky-high rates of incarceration—coupled with onerous sentences and high recidivism—mean that juries may be the only avenue for bringing certain marginalized perspectives into our courts. Further, juries in America are a necessary and meaningful check on the discretion of law enforcement officers.[56] It is perhaps this cultural and empirical reality, more than anything, that has fueled scholarship on the power and potential of the "radical enfranchisement" of jurors to offer a corrective to racial disparities naturalized in (and through) the legal system today.[57]

The stakes are high if our current analytical tools for making sense of juries and their central role in prosecutors' work do not capture their power and complexity.[58] Ethnography is critical for showing empirically how exactly the jury matters—and does not matter—at the federal level in the contemporary United States. In this spirit, legal scholars and reformers should embrace ethnographic research's "regenerative capacity"—as Marilyn Strathern puts it—as it "build[s] up the conditions from which the world can be apprehended anew."[59] Or at least be imagined differently.

ACKNOWLEDGMENTS

I am indebted to the many assistant US attorneys whose insight and intellectual generosity made this book possible. Though anonymization precludes thanking you by name, I acknowledge your incredible contribution to my learning as a legal scholar and anthropologist.

Beyond my interlocutors, this book is a reflection of the remarkable colleagues and friends who participated in its development. I must express my gratitude first to the wonderful community of scholars at Princeton University. First and foremost, I am grateful to Carol J. Greenhouse for her invaluable input, inspiration, and encouragement over the course of this project. Along the way, this study also benefited immensely from the close reading and thought-provoking commentary of Kim Lane Scheppele, Lawrence Rosen, and Richard Wilson. I also thank João Biehl, Jim Boon, John Borneman, Peter Brooks, Lisa Davis, Gabriela Drinovan, Abdellah Hammoudi, Rena Lederman, Serguei Oushakine, Lauren Coyle Rosen, Carolyn Rouse, Mo Lin Yee, and Carol Zanca. And of course there were my wonderful graduate school peers, who discussed various iterations of this project—thank you Avani Mehta Sood, Neel Sukhatme, Kalyani Ramnath, Matthew Birkhold, Jessica Cooper, Maayan Dauber, Ben Johnson, Peter Conti-Brown, Quincy Amoah, Benjamin Fogarty, and Serena Stein. From the Princeton University Center of Human Values I thank Melissa Lane, Merrick Anderson, Emad Atiq, John Peter DiIulio, Emily Kern, Lucia Rafanelli, Paula Vedoveli, and David Zuluaga Martinez.

Beyond Princeton, I was fortunate to have many enriching conversations about my research, each of which has left some impression on this book. Among the legal scholars and anthropologists I must thank for their support and guidance are Annelise Riles, Justin Richland, Elizabeth Mertz, Didier Fassin, Leslie Gerwin, Lisa Miller, Bernadette Meyler, Robert Weisberg, Adriana Petryna, Alma Gottlieb, Austin Sarat, Melissa Schwartzberg, Helena Wulff, Ulf Hannerz, Gerhard Anders, Julia Eckert,

Susan Ellison, Akhil Gupta, Sarah Muir, Michael Frisch, Sam Issacharoff, Ann Southworth, and Stephen Gillers. Throughout its development, this study has benefited enormously from the contributions of jury scholars, including leading members of the Law and Society Association's Collaborative Research Network, "Lay Participation in Legal Systems." In particular, I would like to thank Valerie Hans, Shari Seidman Diamond, Nancy Marder, Catherine Grosso, Paula Hannaford-Agor, Mary Rose, and Sanja Kutnjak Ivkovich, among others. From NYU Law School, I thank Seth Endo and members of the Lawyering Program colloquium. Thank you, also, to members of the Criminal Justice Schmooze hosted by Bruce Green, Rebecca Roiphe, and Ellen Yaroshefsky for feedback on the central themes of this project. In addition to those already named, I am grateful to Jennifer Laurin, Bennett Gershman, Cynthia Godsoe, Tamara Lave, Jenny Roberts, Maybell Romero, Lauren Ouziel, Peter Joy, Anna Roberts, and Samuel Levine for generous engagement with parts of this manuscript.

The ideas for this study also took shape and matured at Georgetown Law—thank you, Robin West, Gregory Klass, David Luban, Naomi Mezey, and all the participants in GULC's Fellows Workshop and Seminar. Thank you, also, to Mike Seidman, who welcomed my participation in Georgetown's Summer Workshop during a key period of research preparation.

While writing this book, I was immensely fortunate to receive and accept an offer to join an incomparable group of legal scholars at Southern Methodist University. I extend my sincere thanks to Jennifer Collins, Joanna Grossman, Jeffrey Kahn, Jenia Turner, Joshua Tate, Meghan Ryan, Kenitra Brown, Chris Jenks, Eric Ruben, Hillel Bavli, Tom Kimbrough, and Greg Ivy, among others. I am also grateful for the essential feedback provided by participants in book workshops hosted by Pamela Metzger and the Deason Criminal Justice Reform Center, and by Lolita Buckner Inness. These workshops were attended by Bennett Capers, Carissa Byrne Hessick, Shima Baradaran Baughman, Julia Simon-Kerr, Jessica Roth, Johannah Cousins, and Kristin Meeks, among others.

I also thank my colleagues in Norway who productively challenged the insights of this research from a comparative perspective during the year I spent at the University of Oslo's Department of Public and International Law. This includes Ulf Stridbeck, Sveinung Sandberg, Thomas

Hylland Eriksen, Cecilia Bailliet, Dina Townsend, Carola Lingaas, Bård Sverre Tuseth, Anniken Sørlie, Anett Beatrix Osnes Fause, and the Narrative Criminology Working Group. I am also grateful to colleagues at the U.S.-Norway Fulbright Foundation for Educational Exchange, including Kevin McGuinness, Rena Levin, and Petter Næss, as well as new colleagues I met as a 2016–17 grantee, including Suzanne Dovi and Marla Clayman.

From the University of Cambridge Department of Anthropology, I thank James Laidlaw, who supervised my master's thesis on the US grand jury system, which helped shape my interest in this subject. For introducing me to anthropology as an eleven-year-old, I am grateful to Susan Springer at the Dalton School.

I am grateful to Jennifer Hammer at NYU Press for guiding me through the creation and publication of this book, as well as the anonymous peer reviewers who generously shared their time and wisdom. Thank you to Alexia Traganas and MJ Devaney for editorial assistance and to SMU Law students Leah Anderson, Brenda Balli, Matthew Mussalli, and Briggs Howe for research support.

This book, and the years of fieldwork underlying it would not have been possible without the love and brilliance of Kelly McKowen, whose unceasing intellectual generosity animated every stage of this project. I have felt lucky, throughout, to have drawn on the encouragement and inspiration of my family: Edmund and Oscar, Aviva, Emily and Ken, Sidney, Avi, Edmund (Sonnenblick) Linda, Caroline, Lily, Jennie, Peter, Ben (Denzer), Trish, Kevin, Kaulin, Becky, Suzie, Tristan, Wyatt, Nick, Abbott, Henry (Van Doren), Henry (Zachs), Charlotte, Adam (Van Doren), Mike, Dara, David, Adam (Offit), Yoni, Meg, Marc, Rachel, Ben (Gold), Suzanne, Andy, Tommy, and many others.

This research was supported in part by Princeton University and the National Science Foundation (SES-1535350). I am also grateful for the funding I received as a Laurance S. Rockefeller Graduate Prize Fellow. To explore the comparative implications of this research in Norway, I received support from the U.S.-Norway Fulbright Foundation and the Lois Roth Endowment. The completion of this manuscript was supported in part by the Maria and Michael Boone Faculty Research Fund and the Charles and Peggy Galvin Endowed Faculty Research Fund at SMU Law.

NOTES

INTRODUCTION

1 On the importance of lay juries to participatory democracy, see, e.g., Levin, "The Federal Jury Selection Act of 1968," 55–56, and Carroll, "The Jury as Democracy," 829. In *Powers v. Ohio*, 499 U.S. 400, 407 (1991), Justice Kennedy wrote for the majority that jury service is a citizen's most "significant opportunity to participate in the democratic process"; Justice Gorsuch quoted this very line early in the seven-to-two majority opinion he authored in *Flowers v. Mississippi*, 588 U.S. ___ (2019), 7.

2 Close to thirty-two million citizens are summoned for jury service each year. See Mize, Hannaford-Agor, and Waters, "The State-of-the-States Survey," 8.

3 See Galanter, "Vanishing Trial," 522–31, for the first in a series of articles that have documented the jury system's decline and described the attenuation of its influence in the legal system; US Courts, Federal Judicial Caseload Statistics Tables (2020), table D-4, records that out of 79,997 total reported federal criminal cases that reached trial in 2020 (resulting in a conviction or an acquittal), 1,219 were tried by juries. Federal cases faced a similar but more precipitous decline; 0.63 percent of federal civil cases were resolved by jury trials in 2017, falling to 0.62 percent in 2018. US Courts, Judicial Facts and Figures (2018), table 4.10, shows that in 2017, 1,812 of 289,595 cases were tried by juries, and in 2018, 1,706 of 275,879 cases were tried by juries.

4 Diamond and Salerno, "Reasons for the Disappearing Jury Trial," 122.

5 Capers, "Against Prosecutors," 1568–70.

6 Geertz, "'From the Native's Point of View,'" 29.

7 Greenhouse, *Praying for Justice*, 82.

8 Yngvesson, *Virtuous Citizens*, 12, 17–19, 21.

9 Wilson, *Incitement on Trial*, 109.

10 Coutin, *Legalizing Moves*, 133.

11 Riles, *Collateral Knowledge*, 65–70. Like Amsterdam, Hertz, Ingold, and others, Riles works to open up technical metaphors. This approach complements the aims of the New Legal Realism movement; see Mertz, Macaulay, and Mitchell, *New Legal Realism*, xv, which articulates some of the key contributions that social science research can make to more traditional forms of legal analysis. This includes the use of a "wide variety of approaches that recognize ... law ... as language/discourse, as institutional practices, as aspirational ideals ... and at-

tend[] to the 'constitutive' role of law, or how legal meaning matters, or how legal actors perform legal practices, or how institutional norms and pressures interact with other factors"; Garth and Mertz, in "Introduction: New Legal Realism at Ten Years and Beyond," 125, note that among the contributions of New Legal Realism has been its acceptance of "'bottom-up' empirical perspectives and methods"; writing on legal knowledge practices in the context of financial market transactions, Riles urges the anthropology of law to go "beyond its lingering addiction to a view of the 'jural' (jural relations, jural personhood) as a matter of rules and norms governing rights and obligations, in contrast to the flexible empirical realities of economic relations" (Riles, "Too Big to Fail," 34).

12   Ochs and Capps, *Living Narrative*, 57–58; Hirsch, *Pronouncing and Persevering*, 19; Borneman, *Belonging in the Two Berlins*, 285; Hall, *Representation*, 235, noting that meaning is generated through interaction with an "Other."

13   Van Cleve, *Crook County*, 143.

14   Van Cleve, 103.

15   Kohler-Hausmann, *Misdemeanorland*, 16.

16   Forman, *Locking Up Our Own*, 9.

17   Van Cleve, *Crook County*, 34–36; Thusi, *The Pathological Whiteness of Prosecution*, 110, observing the dearth of scholarship on "the whiteness of [the] prosecutorial function itself" in favor of an emphasis on racial disparities of criminal defendants.

18   Abramson, *We, the Jury*, 49.

19   Amietta, "Everyday Justice at the Courthouse?," 166, advancing an account of justice as an expression of everyday legal practice that collapses binaristic distinctions "everyday" and institutionalized legal practice, examining "the incorporation of laypersons into the decision of criminal trials as a dynamic assemblage co-produced by formal and informal practices, spatiotemporal conditionings, and different meanings attached to participation and judicial authority by multiple authorized entities." Yngvesson, *Virtuous Citizens*, 12, 17–19, 21.

20   Baughman, "Prosecutors and Mass Incarceration," describes obstacles to studying prosecutors' charging decisions. Murray, "Populist Prosecutorial Nullification," 248–52, discusses some prosecutors' efforts to engage in "*programmatic* prosecutorial nullification"; see also Levin, "Imagining the Progressive Prosecutor," 1417–18; Green and Roiphe, "When Prosecutors Politick," 738–42; and Prosecutorial Charging Practices Project, 2021, SMU Dedman School of Law, Dallas, TX, https://deasoncenter.smu.edu.

21   The US attorney's office grant of permission for my research was no doubt connected to its interest in what I might learn as I spoke to AUSAs with a range of experience. The office also appeared to value my institutional affiliations.

22   It is not uncommon for anthropologists engaged in research within legal and other bureaucratic institutions to accept invitations to carry out uncompensated projects in the course of their study. See, e.g., Van Cleve, *Crook County*, xv; Ho, *Liquidated*, 14; Cabot, *On the Doorstep of Europe*, 13. In my case, this consisted

of keeping notes—when cases proceeded to trial—on how judges in the district managed the jury selection process.

23 Among the subjects prosecutors discussed with me were the types of cases they worked on, the arc of their careers, and what a typical workday in the office looked like.

24 In *Misdemeanorland*, a qualitative study of the New York misdemeanor system, Issa Kohler-Hausmann discusses the role that imagined defendants play in judges' and prosecutors' decision-making. She explains that the "type of offense [a defendant is alleged to have committed] is always evaluated in light of *who* judges or prosecutors think they have in front of them. A turnstile jumping case where the defendant has an extensive history of violent or property crime convictions is likely to be seen as troublesome disregard for society's rules, whereas the same crime by a person without a criminal record might be seen as a minor transgression" (108–9). In this respect, judges' and prosecutors' assessments of defendants' culpability are informed by their interpretations of criminal records as predictions of defendants' future behavior. The opacity of prosecutorial discretion and decision-making has been a recurrent practical and scholarly subject of commentary and critique.

25 Nader, "Up the Anthropologist," 11.

26 Sapignoli and Niezen, "Global Legal Institutions," citing Lie, "Challenging Anthropology"; Jacob and Riles, "New Bureaucracies of Virtue," on the ethnographic turn in international relations.

27 Latour, *Making of Law*, 71.

CHAPTER 1. PROSECUTORIAL DISCRETION

1 See *U.S. Attorney's Manual*, § 9-27.110 (which addresses aspects of prosecutors' work that entail the broad exercise of discretion, including "initiating and declining prosecution," "selecting charges," "entering into plea agreements," "opposing offers to plead nolo contendere," "entering into non-prosecution agreements in return for cooperation," and "participating in sentencing").

2 Prosecutors I spoke with believed this figure was significantly higher in practice, since many routinely fielded preliminary calls from law enforcement agents related to cases they believed did not warrant prosecution at the federal level. See also Motivans, Table 4, "Outcome and Case Processing Time of Suspects in Matters Concluded, FY 2016," in *Federal Justice Statistics, 2016*, 479–80. See Roth, "Prosecutorial Declination Statements," 479–80, who notes that "in an era of expansive criminal law and finite government resources, declinations constitute an ever more significant piece of the criminal justice picture, even if the precise size of that piece is unknown," citing selected studies that estimate anywhere from 4 percent to 50 percent of cases referred to prosecutors are declined, varying by jurisdiction and offense classification (www.bjs.gov, accessed November 10, 2020). This figure also excludes the large number of "uncounted declinations" made by investigative agencies that are not brought to the attention of the US attorney's office. See Miller and Wright, *Criminal Procedures*, 805.

3 Olsen et al., "Collecting and Using Data for Prosecutorial Decisionmaking," 6.

4 Weinberg, "Harmful Error," 30.

5 *U.S. Attorney's Manual*, § 9-27.220, discusses the factors that should inform a prosecutor's decision to take a case, including consideration of whether "(1) the prosecution would serve no substantial federal interest; (2) the person is subject to effective prosecution in another jurisdiction; or (3) there exists an adequate non-criminal alternative to prosecution."

6 See *U.S. Attorney's Manual*, February 2018 (updated), § 9-27.220, on the "grounds for commencing or declining prosecution."

7 See *U.S. Attorney's Manual*, February 2018 (updated), § 9-27.230, on the nature and seriousness of an offense.

8 Spears and Spohn, "Genuine Victim," 183, 197–99, 200–3; Corrigan, *Up against a Wall*, chap. 4; Trivedi and Van Cleve, "To Serve and Protect Each Other," 913; Jackman and Barrett, "Charging Officers with Crimes Is Still Difficult for Prosecutors"; Chemerinsky, "Private."

9 See Lee, *Murder and the Reasonable Man*; Vitiello, "Defining the Reasonable Person," 1443–49; Faulkner, "Dear Courts," 252; Korsmo, "Lost in Translation," 299–301.

10 Federal Rule of Evidence 104(b).

11 Federal Rule of Criminal Procedure 29.

12 See Wilson, *Writing History in International Criminal Trials*, 196, 217; Ochs and Capps, *Living Narrative*; and Richland, *Arguing with Tradition*. See also Coutin, *Legalizing Moves*, 122, for a pertinent discussion of creativity in legal settings based on a study of language in legal settings; Sarat and Felstiner, "Lawyers and Legal Consciousness," 1682, for discussion of the multiple and simultaneous meanings and possibilities of legal language for clients' cases; Cormack, *Power to Do Justice*, 1; Papke *Narrative and the Legal Discourse*, 104; and Shapiro, "On the Regrettable Decline of Law French," 1201. Hall, *Representation*, 235, discusses how meaning is generated through interaction with an "Other." See also Duranti, "The Audience as Co-author," 241; Hill, *Responsibility and Evidence in Oral Discourse*, 4; Bauman, "Verbal Art as Performance," 302; Fox, "Evidentiality," 170; Bakhtin, Wright, and Holquist, *Dialogic Imagination*, 293–94; Hirsch, *Pronouncing and Persevering*, 19; and Jacoby and Ochs, "Co-construction," 175.

13 Sarat and Felstiner, "Legal Realism in Lawyer-Client Communication," 136.

14 Sarat and Felstiner, 148–49.

15 Amsterdam and Hertz, "Analysis of Closing Arguments," 56, emphasize the uncertainty of legal outcomes in a New York homicide prosecution that could "go either way."

16 Strathern, *Gender of the Gift*, 19; Riles, *Collateral Knowledge*, 14.

17 McGranahan, "Anthropology of Lying," 247.

18 Greenhouse, *Praying for Justice*, 33.

19 Geertz, *Local Knowledge*, 233 ("It is doubtful whether the history, sociology, and philosophy of a field are well advised to adopt as their own the sense of it held by

its practitioners, caught up, as those practitioners are, in the immediate necessities of craft"). Riles, *Collateral Knowledge*, 70, 72, notes that informants may understand their techniques as "problem-solving tools," while closer ethnographic examination suggests their techniques operate differently.

20 Among the often cited but rarely elaborated expressions of prosecutors' ethical obligations is found the US Supreme Court's opinion in *Berger v. United States*, which characterized the prosecutor as "the representative not of an ordinary party to a controversy, but of a sovereignty whose . . . interest, therefore, in a criminal prosecution is not that it shall win a case, but that justice shall be done" (295 U.S. 78, 88 [1935]).

21 Bharara, *Doing Justice*, 176.

22 Roberts, "Expunging America's Rap Sheet," 330–35.

23 Baughman, "Prosecutors and Mass Incarceration."

24 Natapoff, *Punishment without Crime*, 71.

25 Natapoff, 71.

26 Natapoff, 233. Throughout this account, Natapoff juxtaposes state and federal court practice. Drawing on her experience as an assistant federal defender in Baltimore, Natapoff writes: "Federal court is the top of the pyramid, there were lots of resources, and everything mattered, even misdemeanors. . . . I had plenty of time to talk to my clients, investigate, and prepare. Every official player in the courtroom—me, the prosecutor, the judge—had the wherewithal to take each case seriously. My office expected me to litigate zealously when issues arose, and the prosecutors and judges expected that to happen. There were motions and hearings and trials and appeals" (248). See also Richman, "Prosecutors and Their Agents," 765, which describes the gatekeeping dynamics between US attorney's offices and other federal law enforcement agencies.

27 See Barkow, *Prisoners of Politics*, 160–63, for a relevant discussion of how state prosecutors, facing election, deploy metrics that fail to promote policies that might enhance public safety, such as working with law enforcement peers to divert resources from low-level cases that exacerbate inequality and increase rates of incarceration.

28 Capers, "Against Prosecutors," 1592; see also Barkow, *Prisoners of Politics*, chap. 8; Bazelon, *Charged*, chap. 14.

29 Pfaff, *Locked In*, chap. 5.

30 Forman, *Locking Up Our Own*, 13–14.

31 Kohler-Hausmann, *Misdemeanorland*, 195; Bellin, "The Power of Prosecutors," 198.

32 Kennedy, "Sentencing Reform Act of 1984," 63; Braniff, "Local Discretion, Prosecutorial Choices," 309; Conrad and Clements, "Vanishing Criminal Jury Trial," 132–36.

33 Bay, "Prosecutorial Discretion in the Post-*Booker* World," 550.

34 Hessick, *Punishment without Trial*, 35–38, describing an illustrative case in which prosecutors offered a defendant a plea deal that "was too good to pass up" in

light of the sentence he might face if convicted by a jury at trial. She notes that "if a prosecutor offers a good enough deal—a plea bargain with a sentence that is significantly less than the expected punishment—then a defendant would have to be crazy to turn it down."

35 Natapoff, *Punishment without Crime*, 55.

36 Van Cleve, *Crook County*, 113, describes an episode in which a defense attorney's advocacy for one client prompts a trial judge to offer a lenient sentence while vowing that the lawyer's *next* client was "going to get it."

37 Baskin and Sommers, "Influence of Forensic Evidence"; Spears and Spohn, "Genuine Victim."

38 Baskin and Sommers, "Influence of Forensic Evidence," 330.

39 Spears and Spohn, "Genuine Victim," 201–2.

40 Davis, *Arbitrary Justice*, 16.

41 Kreag, "Disclosing Prosecutorial Misconduct," 315.

42 In *Brady v. Maryland*, 373 U.S. 83, 83 S. Ct. 1194, 10 L. Ed. 2d 215 (1963), the US Supreme Court held that the prosecutor's failure to volunteer evidence favorable to the defendant upon request is a violation of due process when such evidence is "material either to guilt or to punishment, irrespective of the good faith or bad faith of the prosecution" (1197).

43 Brian A. Reaves, Bureau of Justice Statistics, US Department of Justice, Felony Defendants in Large Urban Counties (2009), Statistical Tables, table 21 (December 2013), www.bjs.gov.

44 Bureau of Justice Statistics, US Department of Justice, Federal Criminal Case Processing Statistics (2014), www.bjs.gov.

45 Flango and Clarke, *Reimagining Courts*, table 4A1.

46 For data from 2020, see US Courts, Federal Judicial Caseload Statistics Tables (2020), table D-4, www.uscourts.gov.

47 Bureau of Justice Statistics, *Federal Justice Statistics* (2012), Statistical Tables, table 4.2 (2015). Guilty pleas constitute 95 percent of state convictions; see Bureau of Justice Statistics, US Department of Justice, *State Court Sentencing of Convicted Felons*, Statistical Tables, table 4.1 (2004).

48 Levenson, "Peeking behind the Plea Bargaining Process," 469–70; Bar-Gill and Ben-Shahar, "The Prisoners' (Plea Bargain) Dilemma," 737.

49 Easterbrook, "Criminal Procedure as a Market System," 303.

50 Bibas, "Transparency and Participation in Criminal Procedure," 951.

51 Turner, *Transparency in Plea Bargaining*, 4 ("The secrecy of the process also raises a number of concerns. First, it prevents adequate oversight of a procedure that has been broadly criticized as enabling coercion, concealment of facts, and disparate treatment. Non-transparency makes it more difficult for defense attorneys to assess the reasonableness of plea offers they receive and to provide fully informed advice to their clients. It can give rise to unnecessary disputes after the fact about the terms of the bargain and the quality of assistance provided by defense counsel. The lack of transparency also frustrates the ability of victims to provide mean-

ingful input, and it leaves judges with few guideposts by which to evaluate the fairness of plea bargains and the validity of guilty pleas").

52 Barrera, *Performing the Court*, 327.

53 Bibas, "Plea Bargaining outside the Shadow of Trial," 2467–68.

54 Bowers, "Plea Bargaining's Baselines," 1101.

55 Natapoff, *Punishment without Crime*, 7, notes that federal system constitutes a gold standard for the criminal justice system relative to the diffuse and overburdened misdemeanor system.

56 Sarat and Clarke, "Beyond Discretion," 391; Bowers, "Legal Guilt, Normative Innocence," 1672.

57 In this article, Sarat and Clarke build on Carl Schmitt's (1985) conception of sovereign power as one who "decides on the exception," focusing on instances of emergency that necessitate decisive action that is out of alignment with legal norms.

58 Collins, "Crime and Parenthood," 828–32. In this original empirical study of prosecutions of parents and guardians in child neglect cases that resulted in death, Collins notes some of the striking disparities, including a "suffering discount" applied to defendants who are parents and preferential treatment based on socioeconomic status.

59 Markel, "Against Mercy," 1478.

60 Capers, "Against Prosecutors," 1565, cites a study of law enforcement officers' decision not to prosecute rape cases between 1995 and 2012. See also Yung, "How to Lie with Rape Statistics," 1237–38.

61 Green and Roiphe, "Fiduciary Theory of Prosecution," 157, articulating a theory of decision-making that acknowledges the "amorphous" and "vague" nature of prosecutors' imperative to seek justice—focusing instead on the process by which prosecutors assign meaning and significance to their duties of care and loyalty.

CHAPTER 2. IMAGINING THE JURY

1 Brunnegger, "Theorizing Everyday Justice," 5–6, is concerned with how "conceptions of justice circulate and change, and how they are imagined, legitimated, and negotiated within particular spatial settings and temporal regimes."

2 Greenhouse, "Afterword," 207, formulating justice "not [as] the preserve of judges alone, as end-points to their deliberations to be reconciled, but as a property of anyone's thinking—or . . . impulses, expressions, episodic before and after the fact, inconsistent, proliferating, condensing," offered definition through "myriad forms of rehearsal, expression, and materialization in the social contexts of their research sites."

3 See Emerson and Paley, "Organizational Horizons and Complaint Filing," 245–46, for a pertinent discussion of the context-specific and contingent character of prosecutorial decision-making: "From the point of view of a decision-maker, relevant 'context' does not stand outside a decision, but is emergent with the shifting, contingent processes of interpretation and judgment that arise in coming to that decision.

Thus, decision-makers do not first determine the 'facts of the case' and then look for 'relevant contextual factors.' Rather 'context' presents itself to decision-makers as horizons of possibilities: as one comes to confront 'a matter needing decision' (itself an evaluative, interpretive, i.e. discretionary process) and begins to weigh alternative ways of proceeding/deciding, one sees at a glance or upon reflection relevant connections, dimensions, implications." One such variable "context" cited by the authors is lawyers' selective reference to attributes of defendants in approaching plea negotiations; see Maynard, *Inside Plea Bargaining*, 138.

4 This approach differs from a horizontal prosecution model in which line attorneys work in units that oversee particular phases of the adjudication process. Purpura, *Criminal Justice*, 216–17.

5 Yaroshefsky and Green, "Prosecutors' Ethics in Context," 282–84; Levine and Wright, "Prosecution in 3D." Current social science and journalistic research suggests that organizational constraints, including the hierarchical character of an office, can limit individual lawyers' autonomy. Supervisors within units and divisions tasked with reviewing, approving, or reallocating work responsibilities are also subject to such constraints. These types of organizational differences vary between offices and districts.

6 Faulk and Brunnegger, "Introduction: Making Sense of Justice," 5, noting that "concepts of justice in practice . . . may (or may not) rely on the justice that the law can provide *but are neither limited to nor fully encompassed by it* [emphasis in original]."

7 See Luban, "The Conscience of a Prosecutor," 15–20, for a discussion of the inchoate nature of prosecutors' directive to "seek justice not victory"; Luban concludes that the requirement that prosecutors avoid *injustice* is a more "useful imperative."

8 An instructive counterpoint to the relationship American federal prosecutors described between their "commitment to professionalism" and discussions of cases in "moral terms" can be seen in Katarina Jacobsson's study of prosecutors in Sweden, "We Can't Just Do It Any Which Way," 55–57.

9 Berger and Luckman, *The Social Construction of Reality*, 54. Reflecting on the role of "imaginary figures" in everyday life and decision-making, the authors highlight the importance of "linguistic objectification" in animating such actors: "As far as social relations are concerned, language 'makes present' for me not only fellowmen who are physically absent at the moment, but fellowmen in the remembered or reconstructed past, as well as fellowmen projected as imaginary figures into the future. All these 'presences' can be highly meaningful, of course, in the ongoing reality of everyday life."

10 Diamond and Salerno, "Reasons for the Disappearing Jury Trial," 159–63; Schwartzberg, "Justifying the Jury," 452–53.

CHAPTER 3. STORIED JUSTICE

1 Richland, *Arguing with Tradition*, 142.

2 Matoesian, *Law and the Language of Identity*, 166; Keane, *Ethical Life*, 78; Ochs *Constructing Social Identity*, 296, Ochs, "Narrative Lessons," 285.

3 Offit, "Peer Review," 180, reports on a prosecutor who describes the average juror as someone who might "go to work every day, have 2.5 kids, drive a Ford Taurus, and have a white picket fence."

4 See Lee, *Murder and the Reasonable Man*, 203, acknowledging the role of disembodied "average" or "reasonable" individuals beyond the context of imagined jurors: "Even though we live in a heterogenous society with peoples of different cultural and religious backgrounds, different income levels, and different outlooks on life, the law assumes the existence of a typical or average person whom it calls the Reasonable Person."

5 Rosen, *Law as Culture*, 9; Lakoff and Johnson, *Metaphors We Live By*, 118; Douglas, *How Institutions Think*, 65.

6 For a pertinent discussion of the relationship between a legal narrative's perceived veracity and lawyers' selective factual emphases, see Scheppele, "Facing Facts in Legal Interpretation," 49: "Behind every description of facts, there are many other versions, equally true but differently organized. Changes in emphasis, alternative points of view, different symbolic contexts, varying background assumptions all have their effects on which version of a particular story seems the most compelling."

7 Polanyi, *Telling the American Story*, 93.

8 Thomas Ugelvik's field research in Oslo Prison, for example, has examined the way that inmates narratively identify themselves as ethical individuals. Ugelvik's research reveals that these narratives were the basis for a collective process of moral "sense making." Ugelvik, "The Rapist and the Proper Criminal," 27; Fleetwood, "In Search of Respectability," 62; "Bruner, "Narrative Construction of Reality," citing Kermode, *The Sense of an Ending*.

9 Jacobsson, "'We Can't Just Do It Any Which Way,'" 63, noting the value of supplementing interview data with observational research.

CHAPTER 4. SELF-CONSCIOUS VOIR DIRE

1 Wright, Chavis, and Parks, "The Jury Sunshine Project," 1411–15; Offit, "Benevolent Exclusion," 627–29.

2 *Batson v. Kentucky*, 476 U.S. 79, articulates a three-step test for adjudicating suspected race-based exclusion. First, following defense counsel's *Batson* challenge, a trial court judge determines whether this challenge is a prima facie case of discrimination by considering whether the juror belongs to a protected class and whether all "relevant circumstances" of the strike raise an inference of impermissible discrimination (96–97). Subject to this finding, the burden shifts to the state

to provide a "neutral explanation" for challenging prospective jurors in question (97). The trial court concludes the inquiry by determining whether the defendant has established purposeful discrimination, thus supporting a *Batson* violation (98).

3 Price, "Performing Discretion or Performing Discrimination," 72.

4 See, e.g., *People v. Smith*, 417 P.3d 662, 681 (Cal. 2018), which, citing *Foster v. Chatman*, 578 U.S. ___136 (2016), notes that this technique "carries a significant danger," namely, that "the trial court will take a shortcut in its determination of the prosecutor's credibility, picking one plausible item from the list and summarily accepting it without considering whether the prosecutor's explanation as a whole, including offered reasons that are implausible or unsupported by the prospective juror's questionnaire and voir dire, indicates a pretextual justification."

5 Bennett, "Unraveling the Gordian Knot," 150; Page, Batson's *Blind-Spot*, 156.

6 See Zalman and Tsoudis, "Plucking Weeds from the Garden," 369: "It seemed to us that several prosecutors, including women and minority attorneys, had internalized the *Batson* ethic and were ethically opposed to removing jurors on the basis of race or gender. (Resp. #13, #20, #29, #36, #49, Pros.) As an indication of the depth of feelings on the issue, a prosecutor reported being so upset at a lengthy *Batson* hearing out of the jury's presence as to ask, 'Judge, are you going to brand me as a racist because I exercised a peremptory?' and was mildly rebuked by the court. (Resp. #49, Pros.) 'I try not to—not just because of *Batson*—I try not to let race influence my decision about jurors.' (Resp. #13, Pros.) One defense attorney did not recall a prosecutor ever removing an African American juror on voir dire. (Resp. #12, Crim. Def.)"

7 One prosecutor I interviewed, for example, characterized the jury selection process as "way out of your control" and likened efforts to make sense of juror responses to reading tea leaves.

8 As Preet Bharara, former US attorney for the Southern District of New York, puts it, "Once the case goes to twelve ordinary Americans, anything can happen" (*Doing Justice*, 279).

9 See Marder, "Juror Bias, Voir Dire," 931, which notes that voir dire in federal court most commonly consists of judge-led questioning.

10 I interviewed a number of federal prosecutors who characterized voir dire in federal court as a "low-information" environment for assessing prospective jurors. In the district in which I conducted my research, standardized jury selection questions included those pertaining to prospective jurors' county of residence, occupations, the occupations of family members living in their households, impressions of and extent of contact with law enforcement agents, education levels, news outlets they followed, and hobbies.

11 Mize and Hannaford-Agor, "Building a Better Voir Dire Process," table 1, reports that voir dire is exclusively or predominantly led by judges 69.6 percent of the time in federal court and that in state court, it is exclusively or predominantly led

by judges 25.9 percent of the time and led by judges and lawyers equally in 19.4 percent of cases.

12 Of the twenty-six jury selection proceedings I observed, four featured adjudicated *Batson* challenges.

13 In this vein, one prosecutor I interviewed recounted learning from a former juror that she disapproved of his wearing mismatched socks and shirts and offered him shopping recommendations.

14 See Offit, "Peer Review," 178–79, in which a prosecutor interviewee commented that the only unpredictable variable during a criminal prosecution was the opinions of jurors: "We don't walk into court unless we know we have all the evidence. . . . [T]he only variable—the only outlier—is the jury. You never know what a jury's going to care about."

15 See Alfieri, "Retrying Race," which discusses the analogous context of prosecutorial exercises of discretion in charging decisions aimed at facilitating the retrial of civil rights cases. A limitation of the instrumentalism that is part of explicitly "dispassionate and objective" approaches to discriminating litigants (or jurors), this study argues, is its "lack [of] candor," which "risks unfairness" to all (1144).

16 See Offit, "Peer Review, 172, which notes prosecutors' shared belief that judicial discretion to determine the quantity and substance of questions posed to jurors limits the information that can be gleaned through the jury selection process.

17 I observed a judge during jury selection proceedings in one case, for example, assign racial identities for each prospective juror on record in the course of adjudicating a *Batson* challenge.

18 See Margolis, "Color as a *Batson* Class in California," 2086–87, which points to the growing rate of biracial identification and the benefit that would be conferred by recognizing "color" rather than race as a class for the purposes of antidiscrimination law.

19 Offit, "Playing by the Rule," 1264.

20 Zalman and Tsoudis, "Plucking Weeds from the Garden," 370–71n14, 370. Zalman and Tsoudis interviewed both criminal and civil litigators for a sample drawn from forty-four trials that took place during consecutive months in the late 1990s.

21 Federal Rules of Criminal Procedure 24; *Hamling v. United States*, 418 U.S. 87, 140, 94 S. Ct. 2887, 2919, 41 L. Ed. 2d 590 (1974). Rule 24 of the Federal Rules of Criminal Procedure, which governs jury selection, is widely interpreted as granting judges broad discretion to determine the parameters and types of questions they ask of prospective jurors.

22 See, e.g., Ark. Code Ann. § 16-31-103, which excuses for cause those who assert that the state of their health requires their absence from jury service, and Conn. Gen. Stat. Ann. § 51-217a, which excuses jurors for cause upon a finding of extreme hardship.

23 In federal court, judges seeking guidance from the US Courts Administrative Office can expect to find little help, as the website notes that written requests for excusal due to "undue hardship or extreme inconvenience" may be honored, but does not offer examples (Administrative Office of the U.S. Courts, "Juror Qualifications," www.uscourts.gov).

24 Offit, "Peer Review," 190.

25 See Tetlow, "Granting Prosecutors Constitutional Rights to Combat Discrimination," 1144–51, for a discussion of inquiries into juror bias during voir dire, which the US Supreme Court has not recognized as a right for prosecutors; Lee, "New Approach to Voir Dire on Racial Bias," 852–60.

26 The US Supreme Court's decision in *Peña-Rodriguez v. Colorado*, which followed the bulk of my fieldwork, creates another impetus for lawyers to consider the role of a juror's racial bias in a criminal case's outcome or possible appeal.

CHAPTER 5. JUDGING CHARACTER

1 For a discussion of the interactive and dynamic process of conversational assessments of others, see Goodwin and Goodwin, "Assessments and the Construction of Context," 162–64. Federal prosecutors' imputations of character traits to imagined jurors are not unlike the "creation of others as 'moral characters' through interactions described by ethnographers in other societal domains (Yerkovich, "Gossiping as a Way of Speaking," 192). See also Haviland, *Gossip, Reputation and Knowledge in Zinacantan*, 157, characterizing gossip as "an activity through which actual behavior is verbally bent into a form amenable to the application of rules."

2 As De Luca and Buell note in "Liars! Cheaters! Evildoers!" (31), "Character becomes important not only for its own sake, or for completion of duties, but because it becomes evidence of the good or evil, normalcy or deviance, of policies promoted by a particular character." According to Redmayne in *Character Evidence in the Criminal Trial*, 196, "When bad character evidence is introduced as evidence of a defendant's lack of credibility, it will almost always involve previous convictions. A key assumption, then, is that there is a connection between criminality—or certain types of criminality—and credibility."

3 See Federal Rule of Evidence 102, which advances rules and procedures aimed at helping jurors in "ascertaining the truth and securing a just determination," and Federal Rules of Evidence 404; for a discussion of prosecutors' impulse to identify defendants in capital cases as possessing the immutable character trait of a "murderer," see Kaufman, *American Roulette*, 133.

4 See Federal Rule of Evidence 404(a)(1); Morris, "Federal Rule of Evidence 404(b)," 181–82; Weissenberger, "Making Sense of Extrinsic Act Evidence," 592–94.

5 Gitchel, "The Admissibility (and Inadmissibility) of Character Evidence," 10.

6 Federal Rule of Evidence 404(b)(1).

7 Simon-Kerr, "Uncovering Credibility," 587.

8 Simon-Kerr, 586, notes that "while the result of having credibility is that one is believed, having credibility is not necessarily a function of truth-telling. One can be lying and still have credibility just as one can lack credibility and be truthful. Instead, credibility attaches to those who comport themselves as though they are truthful."

9 McGranahan, "Anthropology of Lying," 244.

10 Martí, "The Logic of (Mis)Behavior," 473, offers a pertinent discussion of the creation of "outsiders" through "successfully co-constructed criticisms" of others' character through gossip; citing Haviland, *Gossip, Reputation and Knowledge in Zinacantan*, 60.

11 Conley, *Just Words*, 31–37; Matoesian, *Reproducing Rape*, 63; Taslitz, *Rape and the Culture of the Courtroom*, 9–10.

12 Matoesian, *Law and the Language of Identity*, 40, 53.

13 Matoesian, 40, 53, 218, 231, 159.

14 Offit, "With Jurors in Mind," 18.

15 Offit, "Peer Review," 188–89.

16 Offit, 192–93.

17 Adelswärd, "Defendants' Interpretations of Encouragements in Court," 744, observing judges' and prosecutors' comparable practice of relating to defendants who were "first-time offenders, especially those from a middle-class background," with greater compassion and understanding than those who lacked stable employment and "higher social status."

CHAPTER 6. JUDICIAL DISCRETION BEYOND TRUTH

1 Philips, *Ideology in the Language of Judges*, 118–19.

2 Marder, "Juror Bias, Voir Dire," 943, 955.

3 Clark, *American Jury*, 154, for a discussion of practical barriers to judicial neutrality.

4 Philips, *Ideology in the Language of Judges*, 114–15, 123; Hirsch, *Pronouncing and Persevering*, 137.

5 Philips, *Ideology in the Language of Judges*, 92.

CONCLUSION

1 Burns, *Death of the American Trial*, 201.

2 Burns, 211.

3 See, e.g., Jonakait, *American Jury System*, 11.

4 Guinther and Walter, *The Jury in America*, xv.

5 Most recently, see Justice Kennedy's majority opinion (page 2) and Alito's dissent (page 2) in *Pena-Rodriguez v. Colorado* (decided March 6, 2017), www.scotusblog.com. Robert H. Mnookin and Lewis Kornhauser's article "Bargaining in the Shadow of the Law," 997, calls for further empirical attention to how formal legal proceedings influence lawyers' strategy and behavior.

6 See, e.g., DiPerna, *Juries on Trial*, 218.

7 Hans and Vidmar, *American Juries*, 236–40; Clark, *American Jury*, 157–58.

8 Geertz, *Local Knowledge*, 233. Pirie, *Anthropology of Law*, 67–68, suggests that anthropologists have a tendency to examine "what *law does* rather than what *law is*." Foucault, *Order of Things*, 267, discusses an analogous emphasis on function in the development of scientific knowledge.

9 Cormack, *Power to Do Justice*, 1; Shapiro, "On the Regrettable Decline of
Law French," 1201; Sarat and Felstiner, "Lawyers and Legal Consciousness,"
1682; Coutin, *Legalizing Moves*, 122. An analogous discussion of this ends-
focused perspective can be found in Latour's ethnographic work with engi-
neers and laboratory scientists who, for example, concluded that because a
project *did not work*, it *could not have worked*. Latour, *Aramis*, 9, 35, 41, 121.
Latour refers to this mode of assessment as a "retrospective characterization
of facts." Latour and Woolgar, *Laboratory Life*, 190. Pierre Bourdieu has lev-
eled a similar critique of ends-focused approaches to technique by suggesting that they import an *economic* logic of efficiency and "cynical calculating
consciousness" in conditions of openness and uncertainty. Bourdieu, *Practical Reason*, 82–83; Brooks, "Clues, Evidence, Detection," 7–8, critiquing the
narrative logic of the "inevitable discovery" exception to the exclusionary
rule, which assumes a similarly backward-focused approach to evidence
in a criminal case: "Standing at the vantage point of the end of the story,
the proof that the suspect was in fact guilty of illegal activity, the post-hoc
logic of the inevitable discovery doctrine can be used to justify practically
anything—because it is the very logic of narrative, which makes sense by
way of its end. Note that application for a search warrant itself involves
telling the story of what you expect to find in the search—an expectation that then will be confirmed or falsified by the search itself. When you
elide the difference between the standpoint from which you state what you
expect will be the outcome, and the standpoint of the outcome from which
you state that this was what you expected all along, you begin to efface the
difference between the probable—the hypothetical fiction—and the actual.
You confuse the logic of the telling of the story with the putative logic of the
events the story tells"; see also Brooks, "Retrospective Prophecies," 94: "This
sounds to me very much like the logic of a certain kind of narrative explanation that derives beginnings and middles from ends. It is the inferential
logic of the: 'it must have been like this.' It may be the logic of *telling* rather
than of *happening*, and the law can at times confuse the two, turning the
way events are told into the way things happened."

10 Brunnegger, *Everyday Justice*, 4, characterizing recent ethnography as suggesting
that "multiple, often competing, and even incommensurable meanings of justice
operate at different scales and in distinctive forms and interfaces, and different
regimes of justice—both parallel and overlapping—exist within the same cultural
context"; Wilson, *Writing History in International Criminal Trials*, 109; Greenhouse and Kheshti, *Democracy and Ethnography*, 15.

11 Bauman, "Verbal Art as Performance," 302; Yngvesson, *Virtuous Citizens*, 228–30;
Bakhtin, Wright, and Holquist, *Dialogic Imagination*, 293–94.

12 Richland, *Arguing with Tradition*, 118–19.

13 Yngvesson, *Virtuous Citizens*, 12, 17–19, 21.

14 Yngvesson, 22.

15 Yngvesson, 22–23.

16 Richland, *Arguing with Tradition*, 17, 19, 21.

17 Wilson, *Writing History in International Criminal Trials*, 138, 171, 188, 190–91; Greenhouse and Kheshti, *Democracy and Ethnography*, 15.

18 Wilson, 109. See also Yngvesson, *Virtuous Citizens*, 45, who refers to law as a resource subject to varying "deployment in local power struggles."

19 Riles, *Collateral Knowledge*, 65, 70, 229.

20 Brenneis, "Discourse and Discipline at the National Research Council," 32–33.

21 Stark, "Meetings by the Minute(s)," 237.

22 Ingold, *Perception of the Environment*, 413–14; Gershon, "Critical Review Essay," 170; Rorty, *Contingency, Irony, and Solidarity*, 39. See Wilf, "Rituals of Creativity," for a pertinent discussion of technical work's creative dimensions in the context of improvisational musical performance.

23 Illustrative references to this flattened conception of legal technique can be found in Rosen, *Anthropology of Justice*, 59; and Rosen, "Islamic 'Case Law' and the Logic of Consequence," 313.

24 Bashkow, *Meaning of Whitemen*, 146, 249.

25 Binnall, *Twenty Million Angry Men*, for a discussion of the history and impact of felon-juror exclusion statutes.

26 Collins, "Lady Madonna, Children at Your Feet," 150–53, for a discussion of how the romanticization of the parent-child relationship, for example, has resulted in disparities in rates of prosecution and conviction and the leniency of sentences when family members are defendants.

27 Luban, "The Conscience of a Prosecutor," 31.

28 See Sarat and Felstiner, *Divorce Lawyers and Their Clients*, 150–51, for a discussion of an adjacent context of formative interaction between lay and professional legal actors. In reference to attorney-client encounters and conversations, they note that clients bring "matters into the conversation beyond those that are technically relevant and with which lawyers feel comfortable, and they do so even after lawyers think that these matters have been put aside. They do so by resisting recommendations that a lawyer believes are obviously in the client's interest. They do so by pressing lawyers to explain and justify advice given, actions taken, and results produced in light of the client's sense of what is appropriate and fair. Even as they are being 'managed,' clients transform the agendas of lawyers as well as their preferred professional style. Thus, the meaning of professionalism and the nature of professional is challenged at the same time as it is maintained and reproduced." See Wright and Levine, "The Cure for Young Prosecutors' Syndrome," 1099–103, for a pertinent discussion of how prosecutors' experience with jury trials contributed to their "sense of confidence," which the authors attributed to such prosecutors' adoption, in the course of their careers, of a less aggressive or adversarial approach to their work in favor of a more tempered and improvisational one.

29 Hans and Jolivet, "Iron Fist in a Velvet Glove?," 186–87, for a pertinent discussion
of the relationship between the heterogeneity of decision-making bodies and the
character of their deliberations, as well as the impact of audience effects on speak-
ers' presentations to groups; see also Sommers, "On Racial Diversity and Group
Decision Making."

30 Smith, *Theory of Moral Sentiments*, 161–62. Smith's referent in his description of
the judgment of such an impartial spectator is to the practice of imagining how
an external party either *would* judge or *ought* to judge the matter at hand; see
Taslitz, "A Feminist Approach to Social Scientific Evidence," 36–39, for a pertinent
application of the "judicious spectator" to the role of the juror, citing Nussbaum,
Poetic Justice.

31 States that do not compensate jurors for their first day of service include Arizona,
California, Michigan, Utah, North Dakota, and Delaware; states that do not offer
compensation for the first several days of service include Colorado, Connecticut,
Florida, and Massachusetts (State-of-the-States Survey of Jury Improvement Efforts: A Compendium Report, table 7, 12 www.ncsc-jurystudies.org).

32 Jurisdictions that offer token compensation include New Jersey, which pays five
dollars as compensation for each of the first three days of service, and Pennsylvania which pays nine dollars for each of the first three days of service (Jury
Management, National Centers for State Courts, www.ncsc.org).

33 This gender disparity extends to both uncompensated domestic caregiving roles
and compensated positions outside the home. See, e.g., Early Childhood Workforce Index 2020; Barroso and Horowitz, "The Pandemic Has Highlighted Many
Challenges for Mothers"; Buch, "Senses of Care," 638–40.

34 Ritter, "Jury Service and Women's Citizenship," 479.

35 See, e.g., Texas Government Code Annotated § 62.106.

36 Cal. Ct. R. 2.1008 (d)(7); Fla. Stat. § 40.013 (4) (2019); 705 Ill. Comp. Stat. Ann.
305/10.2; S.C. Code Ann. § 14-7-860; Tex. Gov't Code Ann. § 62.106 (2); WY Stat
§ 1-11-104 (a); Ga. Code Ann. § 15-12-1.1 (3); N.J. Rev. Stat. § 2b:20–10(3); Or. Rev.
Stat. § 10.050 (4–5); Va. Code Ann. § 8.01–341.1 (8).

37 Del. Code Ann. tit. 10, § 4511 (b); Haw. Rev. Stat. § 612–6 (9); Idaho Code § 2–212
(3); Ky. Rev. Stat. Ann. § 29A.100; Mont. Code Ann. § 3-15-313 (1); Okla. Stat. tit.
38, § 38–28 (E)(2); S.D. Codified Laws § 16-13-10.4; Colo. Rev Stat. § 13-71–119.5
(2.5); Neb. Rev. Stat. § 25–1601 (1); and Utah Code Ann. § 78B-1–109(1)(a).

38 See Ala. Code § 12-16-63 (b)(2)(a); Alaska Stat. § 09.20.030; Ariz. Rev. Stat. §
21–202 (B)(4)(c)(i); Conn. Gen. Stat. § 51–217 (b); Iowa Code § 607A.6; 14 Me.
Rev. Stat. Ann. tit. 14, § 1213 (2); Mass. Gen. Laws ch. 234a, § 39; Mo. Rev. Stat.
§ 494.430 (1)(4); Nev. Rev. Stat. § 6.030 (1) (c); N.H. Rev. Stat. Ann. § 500-A:11;
N.M. Stat. Ann. § 38-5-2 (C)(1); N.Y. Jud. Law § 517 (2)(c); N.C. Gen. Stat. § 9–6
(a); N.D. Cent. Code § 27–09.1-11 (2); Ohio Rev. Code Ann. § 2313.14 (5); 42 Pa.
Cons. Stat. § 4503 (3); 9 R.I. Gen. Laws § 9-10-9; Vt. Stat. Ann. tit. 4, § 962 (5)
(b); W. Va. Code § 52-1-11 (b); Wis. Stat Ann. § 756.03 (1–2); Ark. Code Ann.

§ 16-31-103; Kan. Stat. Ann. § 43–159; La. Stat. Ann. § 13:3042 (F); Md. Code Ann., Cts. & Jud. Proc. § 8–402 (c) (1–2); Miss. Code Ann. § 13-5-23 (3)(a); Tenn. Code Ann. § 22-1-103 (b)(4); Wash. Rev. Code § 2.36.100; and Ind. Code § 33-28-5-18 (c) (4)(A-C) for exemptions that can be broadly interpreted.

39   Mackenzie Mays, "Mom on Jury Duty Didn't Have Child Care; Judge Asked What If She 'Got Hit by a Mack Truck,'" *Fresno Bee*, December 6, 2018, www.fresnobee.com.

40   In "The Jury Sunshine Project," a North Carolina state court case study, Wright, Chavis, and Parks report that judges and prosecutors removed nonwhite jurors at higher rates than they removed white jurors (1426). They also note that "defense attorneys *nearly* rebalanced the levels of jury service among races by removing more jurors than the judges or the prosecutors did and by using their peremptory strikes more often against white jurors than they did against black and other nonwhite jurors" (1426).

41   See, e.g., *Flowers*, 139 S. Ct. at 2271, which quotes Justice Thomas's comment that he "would return to our pre-*Batson* understanding—that race matters in the courtroom—and thereby return to litigants one of the most important tools to combat prejudice in their cases." See also Smith, "Nice Work If You Can Get It," 528–31, which defends the idea that the racial makeup of the jury is one among other strategic considerations a defense attorney who wants to zealously advocate for their clients ought to be able to consider. In addition, Smith notes, "I have no obligation as an attorney to fight cultural stereotypes unless they are being used against my client, or to serve the interests of the broader community, unless this somehow also serves my client."

42   Price, "Performing Discretion or Performing Discrimination," 61: "Courts' lack of meaningful investigation into prosecutorial motives during *Batson* hearings means that everything short of an explicitly racial statement—e.g., 'I do not want this juror because they are black'—is upheld as race neutral reasoning for exclusion."

43   *Flowers*, 139 S. Ct. 2228 (2019), which discussed the potential for *Batson* to be abused in holding that Mississippi district attorney Doug Evans purposefully excluded Black prospective jurors during voir dire in the capital prosecution of a Black defendant; see also Melilli, "*Batson* in Practice," 489, reports how peremptory rationales, such as assertions that prospective jurors are "'timid,' create an 'unfavorable impression,' 'answered no voir dire questions,' are 'assertive,' are 'liberal or lenient,' are 'eager to serve' or are 'emotional,'" are highly subjective and would be unlikely to precipitate a cause challenge.

44   Lieberman, *Shifting the Color Line*, 7, which suggests that "racial bias in a race-laden policy need not be the result of racism per se." See also Matoesian, "Language, Law, and Society," 682–83n60, for a discussion of the extent to which exclusionary outcomes may result from legal processes that appear superficially agnostic to the racial identities of their participants.

45 Matoesian, "Language, Law, and Society," 683.

46 Binnall, "Summonsing Criminal Desistance," 16–17, which argues by analogy that jurors with felony records feel similarly to those who have been racially prejudiced; being selected for jury service feels like a "show of trust by the state," tempering feelings of social exclusion; and Roberts, "Asymmetry as Fairness," 1523.

47 Gastil et al., *The Jury and Democracy*, 32; Feller, Gastil, and Hans, "Civic Impact of Civil Jury Service," 24, 26. Feller, Gastil, and Hans note that those who deliberated as part of twelve-person unanimous civil jury trials were more likely to vote after completing their service.

48 Diamond, "What Jurors Think," 282, 285.

49 Carissa Byrne Hessick articulates this view succinctly in critiquing the prevalence of plea negotiation as a substitute for the jury trial. She writes, "A system designed to circumvent jury trials actually ends up circumventing other controls on the criminal justice system as well, including the public's sense of right and wrong. Not only is the public not able to understand what the officials are doing in their name, but they are removed as a check in individual cases." See Hessick, *Punishment without Trial*, 182.

50 Fisher, "Jury's Rise as Lie Detector," 705–7: "Whether by tradition or conscious design, the jury's verdict has been largely impenetrable. There never has been a mechanism by which the defendant or anyone outside the system could command the jury to reveal its decisionmaking processes. The jury's secrecy is an aid to legitimacy, for the privacy of the jury box shrouds the shortcomings of its methods."

51 Offit, "The Jury Is Out," 232.

52 Rundberget, "Juryordningen."

53 *Straffeprosessloven* Kap. 24 § 359.

54 *Straffeprosessloven* Kap. 24 § 372.

55 *Straffeprosessloven* Kap. 24 § 376e.

56 A similar rationale was adopted as part of Argentina's recent integration of lay participation into the legal system, as a means to "empower society against the discrete realm of the state, which activists see epitomized in what they depict as overly bureaucratized, elitist, and out-of-touch judicial officials" Amietta, "Everyday Justice at the Courthouse?," 165.

57 Chakravarti, *Radical Enfranchisement in the Jury Room*, 98. In Chakravarti's view, the discretionary nature of jury nullification contributes to the radical enfranchisement of lay participants in the legal system. This view of juror empowerment emphasizes civic education—both before and through the experience of participating as a juror—as well as reflexivity about the verdicts juries rendered. Chakravarti concludes that jurors should have three options when rendering a verdict in criminal cases: guilty, not guilty, and nullify. See Luban, *Lawyers and Justice*, 98–99, for comparative insight into

the jury's role as supplying a vision of "lay equity" in the United States that distinguishes it, for example, from the civil and criminal legal process in Germany.

58 Riles, *Collateral Knowledge*, 148, 119.
59 Strathern, *Gender of the Gift*, 19.

BIBLIOGRAPHY

Abramson, Jeffrey B. *We, the Jury: The Jury System and the Ideal of Democracy: With a New Preface.* Cambridge, MA: Harvard University Press, 1994.

Adair, Jennifer. "Post-verdict Contacts with Jurors by Attorneys." *Journal of Legal Profession* 23 (1998–99): 337–45.

Adelswärd, Viveka. "Defendants' Interpretations of Encouragements in Court: The Construction of Meaning in an Institutionalized Context." *Journal of Pragmatics* 13 (1989): 741–49.

Alfieri, Anthony V. "Retrying Race." *Michigan Law Review* 101 (2003): 1141–200.

Alvarez, Lizette. "Zimmerman Juror Discusses How Verdict Was Reached." *New York Times*, July 15, 2003. www.nytimes.com.

American Bar Association. *American Bar Association Criminal Justice Standards for the Prosecution Function.* 4th ed. www.americanbar.org.

Amietta, Santiago Abel. "Everyday Justice at the Courthouse? Governing Lay Participation in Argentina's Criminal Trials." In *Everyday Justice: Law, Ethnography, Injustice,* edited by Sandra Brunnegger, 161–81. Cambridge: Cambridge University Press, 2019.

Amsterdam, Anthony G., and Randy Hertz. "Analysis of Closing Arguments to a Jury." *New York Law School Law Review* 37, no. 1–2 (1992): 55–121.

Andiloro, Nancy R., Brian D. Johnson, and Besiki Luka Kutateladze. "Opening Pandora's Box: How Does Defendant Race Influence Plea Bargaining?" *Justice Quarterly* 33, no. 3 (2016): 398–426.

Aristotle. *The Art of Rhetoric.* In *The Complete Works of Aristotle: The Revised Oxford Translation,* edited by Jonathan Barnes. Vol. 2. Princeton, NJ: Princeton University Press, 1984.

Arnold, Thurman Wesley. *The Symbols of Government.* New York: Harcourt, Brace and World, 1962.

Bakhtin, Mikhail, Jay Wright, and Michael Holquist. *The Dialogic Imagination: Four Essays.* Austin: University of Texas Press, 1981.

Bar-Gill, Oren, and Omri Ben-Shahar. "The Prisoners' (Plea Bargain) Dilemma." *Journal of Legal Analysis* 1, no. 2 (2009): 737–73.

Barker, Joshua, Erik Harms, and Johan Lindquist. *Figures of Southeast Asian Modernity.* Honolulu: University of Hawai'i Press, 2014.

Barkow, Rachel Elise. *Prisoners of Politics: Breaking the Cycle of Mass Incarceration.* Cambridge, MA: Harvard University Press, 2019.

Barrera, Leticia. "Performing the Court: Public Hearings and the Politics of Judicial Transparency in Argentina." *PoLAR: Political and Legal Anthropology Review* 36, no. 2 (2013): 326–40.

Barroso, Amanda, and Juliana Menasce Horowitz. "The Pandemic Has Highlighted Many Challenges for Mothers, but They Aren't Necessarily New." Pew Research Center. March 17, 2021. www.pewresearch.org/.

Barthes, Roland. *A Barthes Reader*. New York: Hill and Wang, 1983.

Bashkow, Ira. *The Meaning of Whitemen: Race and Modernity in the Orokaiva Cultural World*. Chicago: University of Chicago Press, 2006.

Baskin, Deborah, and Ira Sommers. "The Influence of Forensic Evidence on the Case Outcomes of Rape Incidents." *Justice System Journal* 32, no. 3 (2011): 314–34.

Baughman, Shima Baradaran, "Prosecutors and Mass Incarceration." *USC Law Review*. Forthcoming.

Bauman, Richard. "Verbal Art as Performance." *American Anthropologist* 77, no. 2 (1975): 290–311.

Bay, Norman C. "Prosecutorial Discretion in the Post-*Booker* World." *McGeorge Law Review* 37, no. 4 (2006): 549–76.

Bazelon, Emily. *Charged: The New Movement to Transform American Prosecution and End Mass Incarceration*. New York: Random House, 2019.

Bellin, Jeffrey. "The Power of Prosecutors." *New York University Law Review* 94, no. 2 (2019): 171–212.

Bellin, Jeffrey, and Junichi P. Semitsu. "Widening Batson's Net to Ensnare More Than the Unapologetically Bigoted or Painfully Unimaginative Attorney." *Cornell Law Review* 96, no. 5 (2011): 1075–130.

Bennett, W. Lance. "Unraveling the Gordian Knot of Implicit Bias in Jury Selection: The Problems of Judge-Dominated Voir Dire, the Failed Promise of Batson, and Proposed Solutions." *Harvard Law and Policy Review* 4, no. 1 (2010): 149–72.

Berger, Peter L., and Thomas Luckmann. *The Social Construction of Reality: A Treatise in the Sociology of Knowledge*. New York: Open Road Media, 2011.

Bharara, Preet. *Doing Justice: A Prosecutor's Thoughts on Crime, Punishment, and the Rule of Law*. New York: Knopf, 2019.

Bibas, Stephanos. "Plea Bargaining Outside the Shadow of Trial." *Harvard Law Review* 117, no. 8 (2004): 2464–547.

———. "Transparency and Participation in Criminal Procedure." *New York University Law Review* 81, no. 3 (2006): 911–66.

Binnall, James M. "Summonsing Criminal Desistance: Convicted Felons' Perspectives on Jury Service." *Journal of the American Bar Foundation Law and Social Inquiry* 43, no. 1 (Winter 2018): 4–27.

———. *Twenty Million Angry Men: The Case for Including Convicted Felons in Our Jury System*. Oakland: University of California Press, 2021.

Boatright, Robert. *Improving Citizen Response to Jury Summonses: A Report with Recommendations*. Des Moines, IA: American Judicature Society, 1998.

Borneman, John. *Belonging in the Two Berlins: Kin, State, Nation.* Cambridge: Cambridge University Press, 1992.

Bourdieu, Pierre. *Language and Symbolic Power.* Edited and translated by Gino Raymond and Matthew Adamson. Cambridge, UK: Polity Press, 1991.

———. *Practical Reason: On the Theory of Action.* Cambridge, UK: Polity Press, 1998.

Bowers, Josh. "Legal Guilt, Normative Innocence, and the Equitable Decision Not to Prosecute." *Columbia Law Review* 110, no. 7 (2010): 1655–726.

———. "Plea Bargaining's Baselines." *William and Mary Law Review* 57.3 (2015): 1083–146.

Braniff, William. "Local Discretion, Prosecutorial Choices and the Sentencing Guidelines Local Conditions." *Federal Sentencing Reporter* 5, no. 6 (1992): 309–13.

Brenneis, Donald. "Discourse and Discipline at the National Research Council: A Bureaucratic Bildungsroman." *Cultural Anthropology* 9, no. 1 (1994): 23–36. doi:10.1525/can.1994.9.1.02a00020.

Brooks, Peter. "Clues, Evidence, Detection: Law Stories." *Narrative* 25, no. 1 (2017): 1–27.

———. "Retrospective Prophecies: Legal Narrative Constructions." In *New Directions in Law and Literature,* edited by Elizabeth Anker and Bernadette Meyler, 92–108. New York: Oxford University Press, 2017.

Brown, Darryl K. "Jury Nullification within the Rule of Law." *Minnesota Law Review* 81, no. 5 (1997): 1149–200.

Bruner, Jerome. "The Narrative Construction of Reality." *Critical Inquiry* 18, no. 1 (1991): 1–21.

Brunnegger, Sandra, "Theorizing Everyday Justice." In *Everyday Justice: Law, Ethnography, Injustice,* edited by Sandra Brunnegger, 1–34. Cambridge: Cambridge University Press. 2019.

Buch, Elana. "Senses of Care: Embodying Inequality and Sustaining Personhood in the Home Care of Older Adults in Chicago." *American Ethnologist* 40, no. 4 (2013): 637–50.

Bureau of Justice Statistics. *Federal Case Processing Statistics.* 2014. www.bjs.gov.

———. *Federal Justice Statistics.* 2012. www.bjs.gov.

———. *Felony Defendants in Large Urban Counties.* 2009. www.bjs.gov.

———. *State Court Sentencing of Convicted Felons.* 2004. www.bjs.gov.

Burns, Robert P. *The Death of the American Trial.* Chicago: University of Chicago Press, 2009.

Cabot, Heath. *On the Doorstep of Europe: Asylum and Citizenship in Greece.* Philadelphia: University of Pennsylvania Press, 2014.

Capers, Bennett. "Against Prosecutors." *Cornell Law Review* 105, no. 6 (2020): 1561–610.

Carroll, Jenny. "The Jury as Democracy." *Alabama Law Review* 66, no. 4 (2104): 825–70.

Carson, E. Ann. "Prisoners in 2016." US Department of Justice, Bureau of Justice Statistics NCJ 251149, 2018. www.bjs.gov.

Chakravarti, Sonali. *Radical Enfranchisement in the Jury Room and Public Life.* Chicago: University of Chicago Press, 2020.

Chemerinsky, Erwin. "Private: Prosecuting Police Misconduct" (blog post). American Constitution Society, December 1, 2014. www.acslaw.org.

Childs, William G. "The Intersection of Peremptory Challenges, Challenges for Cause, and Harmless Error." *American Journal of Criminal Law* 27, no. 1 (1999): 49–80.

Clark, John W. *The American Jury: Issues and Commentary*. Dubuque, IA: Kendall Hunt, 2010.

Cobb, Jelani. "Rachel Jeantel on Trial." *New Yorker*, June 27, 2013. www.newyorker.com.

Collins, Jennifer. "Crime and Parenthood: The Uneasy Case for Prosecuting Negligent Parents." *Northwestern University Law Review* 100, no. 2 (2006): 807–56.

——. "Lady Madonna, Children at Your Feet: The Criminal Justice System's Romanticization of the Parent-Child Relationship." *Iowa Law Review* 93, no. 1 (2007): 131–84.

Conley, John M., and William O'Barr. *Just Words: Law, Language, and Power*. 2nd ed. Chicago: University of Chicago Press, 2005.

——. *Rules versus Relationships: The Ethnography of Legal Discourse*. Chicago: University of Chicago Press, 1990.

Conley, John M., William O'Barr, and Robin Conley Riner. *Just Words: Law, Language, and Power*. 3rd ed. Chicago: University of Chicago Press, 2019.

Conley, Robin. *Confronting the Death Penalty: How Language Influences Jurors in Capital Cases*. New York: Oxford University Press, 2016.

Conrad, Robert James, and Katy Lynn Clements. "The Vanishing Criminal Jury Trial: From Trial Judges to Sentencing Judges." *George Washington Law Review* 86, no. 1 (2017): 99–167.

Cormack, Bradin. *Power to Do Justice: Jurisdiction, English Literature, and the Rise of Common Law, 1509–1625*. Chicago: University of Chicago Press, 2008.

Corrigan, Rose. *Up against a Wall: Rape Reform and the Failure of Success*. New York: New York University Press, 2013.

Coutin, Susan Bibler. *Legalizing Moves: Salvadoran Immigrants' Struggle for U.S. Residency*. Ann Arbor: University of Michigan Press, 2000.

Cox, Alexandra, and Dwayne Betts. "Mercy towards Decarceration: Examining the Legal Constraints on Early Release from Prison." *Incarceration* 2, no. 1 (2020): 1–14.

Davis, Angela J. *Arbitrary Justice: The Power of the American Prosecutor*. New York: Oxford University Press, 2007.

De Luca, Tom, and John Buell. *Liars! Cheaters! Evildoers! Demonization and the End of Civil Debate in American Politics*. New York: New York University Press, 2005.

Demleitner, Nora V. "Revisiting the Role of Federal Prosecutors in Times of Mass Imprisonment." *Federal Sentencing Reporter* 30, no. 3 (2018): 165–70.

Devers, Lindsey. *Plea and Charge Bargaining: Research Summary*. Washington, DC: Bureau of Justice Assistance, 2011.

Diamond, Shari Seidman. "Beyond Fantasy and Nightmare: A Portrait of the Jury." *Buffalo Law Review* 54, no. 3 (2006): 717–63.

——. "What Jurors Think: Expectations and Reactions of Citizens Who Serve as Jurors." In *Verdict: Assessing the Civil Jury System*, edited by Robert E. Litan, 282–305. Washington, DC: Brookings Institution Press, 1993.

Diamond, Shari, Leslie Ellis, and Elisabeth Schmidt. "Realistic Responses to the Limitations of *Batson v. Kentucky.*" *Cornell Journal of Law and Public Policy* 7, no. 1 (1997): 77–96.

Diamond, Shari Seidman, and Jessica Salerno. "Reasons for the Disappearing Jury Trial." *Louisiana Law Review* 81, no. 1 (2020): 120–63.

DiPerna, Paula. *Juries on Trial: Faces of American Justice.* New York: Dembner Books, 1984.

Douglas, Mary. *How Institutions Think.* Syracuse, NY: Syracuse University Press, 1986.

Dunn, Karlene S. "When Can an Attorney Ask: 'What Were You Thinking?'—Regulation of Attorney Post-trial Communication with Jurors after *Commission for Lawyer Discipline v. Benton.*" *South Texas Law Review* 40 (Fall 1999): 1069–114.

Duranti, Alessandro. "The Audience as Co-author: An Introduction." *Text: Interdisciplinary Journal for the Study of Discourse* 6, no. 3 (1986): 239–47.

———. *A Companion to Linguistic Anthropology.* New York: Wiley, 2004.

Dzur, Albert W. *Punishment, Participatory Democracy, and the Jury.* New York: Oxford University Press, 2012.

Early Childhood Workforce Index 2020. Center for the Study of Child Care Employment, University of California, Berkeley. https://cscce.berkeley.edu/.

Easterbrook, Frank H. "Criminal Procedure as a Market System." *Journal of Legal Studies* 12 (1983): 289–332.

Edelman, Gilad. "Why Is It So Easy for Prosecutors to Strike Black Jurors?" *New Yorker*, June 5, 2015.

Editorial Board. "Excluding Blacks from Juries." *New York Times*, November 2, 2015. www.nytimes.com.

Edwards, Jeanette, Angelique Haugerud, and Shanti Parikh. "The 2016 Brexit Referendum and the Trump Election." *American Ethnologist* 44, no. 2 (2017): 195–200.

Emerson, Robert M., and Blair Paley. "Organizational Horizons and Complaint Filing." In *The Uses of Discretion*, edited by K. Hawkins. Oxford: Clarendon Press, 1994.

Erickson, Bonnie, E. Allan Lind, Bruce C Johnson, and William M. O'Barr. "Speech Style and Impression Formation in a Court Setting: The Effects of 'Powerful' and 'Powerless' Speech." *Journal of Experimental Social Psychology* 14, no. 3 (1978): 266–79.

Ewick, Patricia, and Susan S. Silbey. *The Common Place of Law: Stories from Everyday Life.* Chicago: University of Chicago Press, 1998.

Fairfax, Roger A., Jr. "The Smart on Crime Prosecutor." *Georgetown Journal of Legal Ethics* 25, no. 4 (2012): 905–12.

Faulk, Karen Ann, and Sandra Brunnegger. "Introduction: Making Sense of Justice." In *A Sense of Justice: Legal Knowledge and Lived Experience in Latin America*, edited by Sandra Brunnegger and Karen Ann Faulk, 1–21. Stanford, CA: Stanford University Press, 2016.

Faulkner, Marvel L. "Dear Courts: I, Too, Am a Reasonable Man." *Pepperdine Law Review* 48, no. 1 (2021): 223–60. https://digitalcommons.

Feller, Traci, John Gastil, and Valerie Hans. "The Civic Impact of Civil Jury Service." *Voir Dire* 23, no. 2 (2016): 23–27.

Ferguson, Andrew G. *Why Jury Duty Matters: A Citizen's Guide to Constitutional Action.* New York: New York University Press, 2013.

Ferrara, David. "'We've Heard Every Excuse for Ducking Jury Service' Nevada Judges Say." *Las Vegas Review Journal,* September 27, 2016. www.reviewjournal.com.

Fisher, George. "The Jury's Rise as Lie Detector." *Yale Law Journal* 107 (1997): 575–713.

Flango, Victor E., and Thomas M. Clarke. *Reimagining Courts: A Design for the Twenty-First Century.* Philadelphia: Temple University Press, 2015.

Fleetwood, Jennifer. "In Search of Respectability: Narrative Practice in a Women's Prison in Quito, Ecuador." In *Narrative Criminology: Understanding Stories of Crime,* edited by Lois Presser and Sveinung Sandberg, 42–68. New York: New York University Press, 2015.

Forman, James. *Locking Up Our Own: Crime and Punishment in Black America.* New York: Farrar, Straus and Giroux, 2017.

Foucault, Michel. *The Order of Things: An Archaeology of Human Sciences.* New York: Knopf, 2012.

Fox, Barbara A. "Evidentiality: Authority, Responsibility, and Entitlement in English Conversation." *Journal of Linguistic Anthropology* 11, no. 2 (2001): 167–92.

Fukurai, Hiroshi, Edgar W. Butler, and Richard Krooth. *Race and the Jury: Racial Disenfranchisement and the Search for Justice.* New York: Plenum, 1993.

Galanter, Marc. "The Vanishing Trial: An Examination of Trials and Related Matters in Federal and State Courts." *Journal of Empirical Legal Studies* 1, no. 3 (2004): 459–570.

Garth, Bryant, and Elizabeth Mertz. "Introduction: New Legal Realism at Ten Years and Beyond." *UC Irvine Law Review* 6 (2016): 121–35.

Gastil, John, E. Pierce Deese, Philip J. Weiser, and Cindy Simmons. *The Jury and Democracy: How Jury Deliberation Promotes Civic Engagement and Political Participation.* Oxford: Oxford University Press, 2010.

Geertz, Clifford. "'From the Native's Point of View': On the Nature of Anthropological Understanding. *Bulletin of the American Academy of Arts and Sciences* 28, no. 1 (1974): 26–45.

———. *Local Knowledge: Further Essays in Interpretive Anthropology.* 3rd ed. New York: Basic Books, 2000.

Gershon, Ilana. "Critical Review Essay: Studying Cultural Pluralism in Courts versus Legislatures." *PoLAR: Political and Legal Anthropology Review* 34, no. 1 (2011): 155–74. doi:10.1111/j.1555-2934.2011.01144.x.

Gilles, Myriam. "Class Warfare: The Disappearance of Low-Income Litigants from the Civil Docket." *Emory Law Journal* 65, no. 6 (2016): 1531–68.

Gitchel, Dent. "The Admissibility (and Inadmissibility) of Character Evidence." *Arkansas Lawyer* 47, no. 4 (2012): 10–15.

Goffman, Erving. *The Presentation of Self in Everyday Life.* New York: Doubleday, 1990.

Goodwin, Charles, and Marjorie Goodwin. "Assessments and the Construction of Context." In *Rethinking Context: Language as an Interactive Phenomenon,* edited by Alessandro Duranti and Charles Goodwin, 147–89. Cambridge: Cambridge University Press, 1992.

Green, Bruce, and Rebecca Roiphe. "A Fiduciary Theory of Prosecution." *American University Law Review* 69 (2020): 101–58. https://papers.ssrn.com.

———. "When Prosecutors Politick: Progressive Law Enforcers Then and Now." *Journal of Criminal Law and Criminology* 110, no. 4 (2020): 719–68.

Greenhouse, Carol J. "Afterword." In *Everyday Justice: Law, Ethnography, Injustice*, edited by Sandra Brunnegger, 206–17. Cambridge: Cambridge University Press, 2019.

———. *Praying for Justice: Faith, Order, and Community in an American Town*. Ithaca, NY: Cornell University Press, 1986.

Greenhouse, Carol J., and Roshanak Kheshti. *Democracy and Ethnography: Constructing Identities in Multicultural Liberal States*. Albany, NY: SUNY Press, 1998.

Greenhouse, Linda. "The Supreme Court's Gap on Race and Juries." *New York Times*, August 6, 2015. www.nytimes.com.

Gribaldo, Alessandra. "The Burden of Intimate Partner Violence: Evidence, Experience, and Persuasion." *PoLAR: Political and Legal Anthropology Review* 42, no. 2 (2019): 283–97.

Guinther, John, and Bettyruth Walter. *The Jury in America*. New York: Facts on File, 1988.

Hall, Stuart, ed. *Representation: Cultural Representations and Signifying Practices*. London: Sage Publications in Association with Open University, 1997.

Hans, Valerie P., and Anne Jolivet. "Iron Fist in a Velvet Glove? Judicial Behavior in Mixed Courts." In *Comparative Law and Economics*, edited by Theodore Eisenberg and Giovanni B. Ramello, 182–205. Cheltenham, UK: Edward Elgar Publishing, 2016.

Hans, Valerie, and Neil Vidmar. *Judging the Jury*. New York: Plenum, 1986.

Haviland, John B. *Gossip, Reputation and Knowledge in Zinacantan*. Chicago: University of Chicago Press, 1977.

Hessick, Carissa Byrne. *Punishment without Trial: Why Plea Bargaining Is a Bad Deal*. New York: Abrams, 2021.

Hill, Jane H. *Responsibility and Evidence in Oral Discourse*. Cambridge: Cambridge University Press, 1993.

Hirsch, Susan F. *Pronouncing and Persevering: Gender and the Discourses of Disputing in an African Islamic Court*. Chicago: University of Chicago Press, 1998.

Hlavka, Heather, and Sameena Mulla. "'That's How She Talks': Animating Text Message Evidence in the Sexual Assault Trial." *Law and Society Review* 52, no. 2 (2018): 401–35.

Ho, Karen. *Liquidated: An Ethnography of Wall Street*. Durham, NC: Duke University Press, 2009.

Hoffman, Morris B. "Peremptory Challenges Should Be Abolished." *University of Chicago Law Review* 64, no. 3 (1997): 809–71.

Ingold, Tim. *The Perception of the Environment: Essays on Livelihood, Dwelling and Skill*. London: Routledge, 2000.

Jackman, Tom, and Devlin Barrett. "Charging Officers with Crimes Is Still Difficult for Prosecutors." *Washington Post*, March 29, 2020. www.washingtonpost.com.

Jacob, Marie-Andre, and Annelise Riles. "The New Bureaucracies of Virtue: Introduction." *PoLAR: Political and Legal Anthropology Review* 30, no. 2 (2007): 181–91.

Jacobsson, Katarina. "'We Can't Just Do It Any Which Way': Objectivity Work among Swedish Prosecutors." *Qualitative Sociology Review* 4, no. 1 (2008): 46–67.

Jacoby, Sally, and Elinor Ochs. "Co-construction: An Introduction." *Research on Language and Social Interaction* 28, no. 3 (1995): 171–83.

Johnson, Vida B. "Arresting Batson: How Striking Jurors Based on Arrest Records Violates *Batson*." *Yale Law and Policy Review* 34, no. 2 (2016): 387–424.

Jonakait, Randolph N. *The American Jury System*. New Haven, CT: Yale University Press, 2006.

Kaufman, Sarah Beth. *American Roulette: The Social Logic of American Death Penalty Sentencing Trials*. Oakland: University of California Press, 2020.

Keane, Webb. *Ethical Life: Its Natural and Social Histories*. Princeton, NJ: Princeton University Press, 2016.

Kennedy, Edward M. "Sentencing Reform Act of 1984." *Federal Bar News and Journal* 32, no. 1 (1985): 62–67.

Kerber, Linda K. *No Constitutional Right to Be Ladies: Women and the Obligations of Citizenship*. New York: Hill and Wang, 1999.

Kermode, Frank. *The Sense of an Ending: Studies in the Theory of Fiction*. New York: Oxford University Press, 1967.

Kohler-Hausmann, Issa. *Misdemeanorland: Criminal Courts and Social Control in an Age of Broken Windows Policing*. Princeton, NJ: Princeton University Press, 2018.

Korsmo, Charles R. "Lost in Translation: Law, Economics, and Subjective Standards of Care in Negligence Law." *Penn State Law Review* 118, no. 2 (2013): 285–337. www.pennstatelawreview.org.

Kreag, Jason. "Disclosing Prosecutorial Misconduct." *Vanderbilt Law Review* 72, no. 1 (2019): 297–352.

Lakoff, George, and Mark Johnson. *Metaphors We Live By*. Chicago: University of Chicago Press, 1980.

Langbein, John H. "Understanding the Short History of Plea Bargaining." *Law and Society Review* 13, no. 2 (1979): 261–72.

Lat, David. "Tropical Depression: The Latest in 'Clerkship Lit.'" *Above the Law*, March 22, 2011. https://abovethelaw.com.

Latour, Bruno. *The Making of Law: An Ethnography of the Conseil d'Etat*. Malden, MA: Polity Press, 2010.

———. *Aramis or the Love of Technology*. Translated by Catherine Porter. Camebridge, MA: Harvard University Press, 1996.

Latour, Bruno, and Steve Woolgar. *Laboratory Life: The Construction of Scientific Facts*. Princeton, NJ: Princeton University Press, 2013.

Lee, Cynthia. *Murder and the Reasonable Man: Passion and Fear in the Criminal Courtroom*. New York: New York University Press, 2003.

———. "A New Approach to Voir Dire on Racial Bias." *UC Irvine Law Review* 5, no. 4 (2015): 843–72.

Lenoir, Timothy. *Instituting Science: The Cultural Production of Scientific Disciplines.* Stanford, CA: Stanford University Press, 1997.

Levenson, Laurie L. "Peeking behind the Plea Bargaining Process: *Missouri v. Frye* and *Lafler v. Cooper* Supreme Court—October Term 2011." *Loyola Law Review* 46, no. 2 (2013): 469–70.

Levin, Benjamin. "Imagining the Progressive Prosecutor." *Minnesota Law Review* 105, no. 3 (2021): 1415–51.

Levin, Jeffrey L. "The Federal Jury Selection Act of 1968: A Critique Note." *Columbia Survey of Human Rights Law* 2, no. 1 (1969): 52–90.

Levin, Leslie C., and Lynn Mather. *Lawyers in Practice: Ethical Decision Making in Context.* Chicago: University of Chicago Press, 2012.

Levine, Kate. "Who Shouldn't Prosecute the Police." *Iowa Law Review* 101 (2016): 1447–96. https://ilr.law.uiowa.edu.

Levine, Kay L., and Ronald F. Wright. "Prosecution in 3D." *Journal of Criminal Law and Criminology* 102, no. 4 (2013): 1119–80.

Lévi-Strauss, Claude. "The Structural Study of Myth." *Journal of American Folklore* 68, no. 270 (1955): 428–44.

Lie, Jon Harald Sande. "Challenging Anthropology: Anthropological Reflection on the Ethnographic Turn in International Relations." *Millennium: Journal of International Studies* 41, no. 2 (2013): 201–20.

Lieberman, Robert C. *Shifting the Color Line, Race and the American Welfare State.* Cambridge, MA: Harvard University Press, 2001.

Lopez, German, "Jury Nullification: How Jurors Can Stop Unfair and Racist Laws in the Courtroom." *Vox,* May 2, 2016. www.vox.com.

Luban, David. "The Conscience of a Prosecutor." *Valparaiso University Law Review* 45 (2010): 1–31.

———. *Lawyers and Justice: An Ethical Study.* Princeton, NJ: Princeton University Press, 1988.

MacIntyre, Alasdair. *After Virtue.* Notre Dame, IN: University of Notre Dame Press, 1984.

Marder, Nancy S. "*Batson* Revisited." *Iowa Law Review* 97, no. 5 (2012): 1585–612.

———. "Beyond Gender: Peremptory Challenges and the Roles of the Jury." *Texas Law Review* 73, no. 3 (1995): 1041–138.

———. "Juror Bias, Voir Dire, and the Judge-Jury Relationship." *Chicago-Kent Law Review* 90, no. 3 (2015): 927–56.

Margolis, Emily Rose. "Color as a *Batson* Class in California." *California Law Review* 106, no. 6 (2018): 2067–98.

Markel, Dan. "Against Mercy." *Minnesota Law Review* 88 (2004): 1421–80.

Martí, Alethea F. "The Logic of (Mis)Behavior: Peer Socialization through Assessments among Zinacantec Youth." *Journal of Latin American and Caribbean Anthropology* 18 (2013): 465–84.

Matoesian, Gregory M. "Language, Law, and Society: Policy Implications of the Kennedy Smith Rape Trial." *Law & Society Review* 29, no. 4 (1995): 669–702.

———. *Law and the Language of Identity: Discourse in the William Kennedy Smith Rape Trial.* New York: Oxford University Press, 2001.

———. *Reproducing Rape: Domination through Talk in the Courtroom.* Cambridge, UK: Polity Press, 1993.

Maynard, Douglas W. *Inside Plea Bargaining: The Language of Negotiation.* New York: Plenum, 1984.

McCoy, Candace. "Prosecution." In *The Oxford Handbook of Crime and Criminal Justice*, edited by Michael Tonry, 663–95. Oxford: Oxford University Press, 2011.

McGranahan, Carole. "An Anthropology of Lying: Trump and the Political Sociality of Moral Outrage." *American Ethnologist* 44, no. 2 (2017): 243–48.

Melilli, Kenneth J. "*Batson* in Practice: What We Have Learned about Batson and Peremptory Challenges." *Notre Dame Law Review* 71 (1996): 447–503.

Merry, Sally Engle. *Getting Justice and Getting Even: Legal Consciousness among Working-Class Americans.* Chicago: University of Chicago Press, 1990.

Mertz, Elizabeth, Stewart Macaulay, and Thomas W. Mitchell, eds. *The New Legal Realism.* Vol. 1, *Translating Law-and-Society for Today's Legal Practice.* Cambridge: Cambridge University Press, 2016.

Miller, Marc L., and Ronald F. Wright. *Criminal Procedures: Cases, Statutes, and Executive Materials.* 2nd ed. Alphen aan den Rijn, Netherlands: Wolters Kluwer, 2003.

Mitchell, W. J. T. *On Narrative.* Chicago: University of Chicago Press, 1981.

Mize, Gregory E., and Paula Hannaford-Agor. "Building a Better Voir Dire Process." *Judges' Journal* 47, no. 1 (Winter 2008): 1–6.

Mize, Gregory E., Paula Hannaford-Agor, and Nicole Waters. "The State-of-the-States Survey of Jury Improvement Efforts." National Center for State Courts, 2007.

Mnookin, Robert H., and Lewis Kornhauser. "Bargaining in the Shadow of the Law: The Case of Divorce." *Yale Law Journal* 88, no. 5 (1979): 950–97.

Morris, Andrew J. "Federal Rule of Evidence 404(b): The Fictitious Ban on Character Reasoning from Other Crime Evidence." *Review of Litigation* 17 (1998): 181–208.

Motivans, Mark. *Federal Justice Statistics, 2016.* Washington, DC: Bureau of Justice Statistics, January 2019.

Murray, Kerrel. "Populist Prosecutorial Nullification." *New York University Law Review* 96, no. 1 (2021): 173–255.

Nader, Laura. "Up the Anthropologist: Perspectives Gained from Studying Up." Unpublished paper, 1972. https://eric.ed.gov.

Natapoff, Alexandra. *Punishment without Crime: How Our Massive Misdemeanor System Traps the Innocent and Makes America More Unequal.* New York: Basic Books, 2018.

Ng, Kwai Hang *The Common Law in Two Voices: Language, Law, and the Postcolonial Dilemma in Hong Kong.* Stanford, CA: Stanford University Press, 2009.

Nussbaum, Martha. *Poetic Justice: The Literary Imagination and Public Life.* Boston: Beacon Press, 1995.

O'Barr, William M. *Linguistic Evidence: Language, Power, and Strategy in the Courtroom.* New York: Academic Press, 1983.

Ochs, Elinor. "Constructing Social Identity: A Language Socialization Perspective." *Research on Language and Social Interaction* 26, no. 3 (1993): 287–306.

———. "Narrative Lessons." In *A Companion to Linguistic Anthropology*, edited by Alessandro Duranti, 269–89. Oxford: Blackwell, 2005.

Ochs, Elinor, and Lisa Capps. *Living Narrative: Creating Lives in Everyday Storytelling.* Cambridge, MA: Harvard University Press, 2009.

Offit, Anna. "Benevolent Exclusion." *Washington Law Review.* 96, no. 2 (2021): 613–66.

———. "Ethical Guidance for a Grander Jury." *Georgetown Journal of Legal Ethics* 24 (Summer 2011): 761–81.

———. "The Jury Is Out: An Ethnographic Study of Lay Participation in the Norwegian Legal System." *PoLAR: Political and Legal Anthropology Review* 41, no. 2 (2018): 231–46.

———. "Peer Review: Navigating Uncertainty in the United States Jury System." *UC Irvine Law Review* 6, no. 2 (2016): 169–206.

———. "Playing by the Rule: How ABA Model Rule 8.49(G) Can Regulate Jury Exclusion." *Fordham Law Review* 89, no. 4 (2020): 1257–63.

———. "With Jurors in Mind: An Ethnographic Study of Prosecutors' Narratives." *Law, Culture and the Humanities* (2017). https://doi.org/10.1177/1743872117717426.

Olsen, Robin, Leigh Courtney, Chloe Warnberg, and Julie Samuels. "Collecting and Using Data for Prosecutorial Decisionmaking." Urban Institute, September 2018. www.urban.org.

Page, Antony. "*Batson's* Blind-Spot: Unconscious Stereotyping and the Peremptory Challenge." *Boston University Law Review* 85 (2005): 155–262.

Papke, David Ray. *Narrative and the Legal Discourse: A Reader in Storytelling and the Law.* Liverpool: Deborah Charles, 1991.

Pfaff, John. *Locked In: The True Causes of Mass Incarceration—and How to Achieve Real Reform.* New York: Basic Books, 2017.

Philips, Susan U. "Contextual Variation in Courtroom Language Use: Noun Phrases Referring to Crimes." *International Journal of the Sociology of Language* 49, no. 1 (1984): 29–50.

———. *Ideology in the Language of Judges: How Judges Practice Law, Politics, and Courtroom Control.* Oxford: Oxford University Press, 1998.

Pirie, Fernanda. *The Anthropology of Law.* Oxford: Oxford University Press, 2013.

Polanyi, Livia. *Telling the American Story: A Structural and Cultural Analysis of Conversational Storytelling.* New York: Ablex, 1985.

Pollitt, Daniel R., and Brittany P. Warren. "Thirty Years of Disappointment: North Carolina's Remarkable Appellate *Batson* Record." *North Carolina Law Review* 94, no. 6 (2016): 1957–95.

Powell, Amber Joy, Heather Hlavka, and Sameena Mulla. "Intersectionality and Credibility in Child Sexual Assault Trials." *Gender and Society* 31, no. 4 (2017): 457–80.

Price, Melynda J. "Performing Discretion or Performing Discrimination: Race, Ritual, and Peremptory Challenges in Capital Jury Selection." *Michigan Journal of Race and Law* 15, no. 1 (2009): 57–107.

Provine, Doris Marie. *Judging Credentials: Nonlawyer Judges and the Politics of Professionalism*. Chicago: University of Chicago Press, 1986.

Purpura, Philip. *Criminal Justice: An Introduction*. Boston: Butterworth-Heinemann. 1997.

Redmayne, Mike. *Character Evidence in the Criminal Trial*. Oxford: Oxford University Press, 2015.

Rees, Gethin. "'It Is Not for Me to Say Whether Consent Was Given or Not': Forensic Medical Examiners' Construction of 'Neutral Reports' in Rape Cases." *Social and Legal Studies* 19, no. 3 (2010): 371–86.

Richland, Justin B. *Arguing with Tradition: The Language of Law in Hopi Tribal Court*. Chicago: University of Chicago Press, 2008.

Richman, Daniel. "Prosecutors and Their Agents, Agents and Their Prosecutors." *Columbia Law Review* 103, no. 4 (2003): 749–832.

Riles, Annelise. *Collateral Knowledge: Legal Reasoning in the Global Financial Markets*. Chicago: University of Chicago Press, 2011.

———. "Too Big to Fail." In *Recasting Anthropological Knowledge*, edited by Jeanette Edwards and Maja Petrović-Šteger, 31–48. Cambridge: Cambridge University Press, 2011.

Ritter, Gretchen. "Jury Service and Women's Citizenship before and after the Nineteenth Amendment." *Law and History Review* 20, no. 3 (2002): 479–515.

Roberts, Anna. "Asymmetry as Fairness: Reversing a Peremptory Trend." *Washington University Law Review* 92 (2015): 1503–50.

Roberts, Jenny. "Expunging America's Rap Sheet in the Information Age" *Wisconsin Law Review* 2015, no. 2 (2015): 321–47.

Rorty, Richard. *Contingency, Irony, and Solidarity*. Cambridge: Cambridge University Press, 1989.

Rose, Mary R., and Shari Seidman Diamond. "Judging Bias: Juror Confidence and Judicial Rulings on Challenges for Cause." *Law and Society Review* 42, no. 3 (2008): 513–49.

Rose, Mary R., Shari Seidman Diamond, and Marc A. Musick. "Selected to Serve: An Analysis of Lifetime Jury Participation." *Journal of Empirical Legal Studies* 9, no. 1 (2012): 33–55.

Rosen, Lawrence. *The Anthropology of Justice: Law as Culture in Islamic Society*. Cambridge: Cambridge University Press, 1989.

———. "Islamic 'Case Law' and the Logic of Consequence." In *History and Power in the Study of Law: New Directions in Legal Anthropology*, edited by June Starr and Jane Fishburne Collier, 302–19. Ithaca, NY: Cornell University Press, 1989.

———. *Law as Culture: An Invitation*. Princeton, NJ: Princeton University Press. 2006.

Roth, Jessica. "Prosecutorial Declination Statements." *Journal of Criminal Law and Criminology* 110, no. 3 (2020): 479–549.

Roudik, Peter. "Georgia: Courts with Jurors Established Nationwide." *Global Legal Monitor*, November 9, 2011. www.loc.gov.

Rubenstein, Arie M. "Verdicts of Conscience: Nullification and the Modern Jury Trial." *Columbia Law Review* 106, no. 4 (2006): 959–93.

Rundberget, Aage. "Juryordningen: En Symbolsak Står for Fall." *Meninger*, February 3, 2017. www.adressa.no.

Sandberg, Sveinung. "The Importance of Stories Untold: Life-Story, Event-Story and Trope." *Crime, Media, Culture* 12, no. 2 (2015): 153–71. https://doi.org/10.1177/1741659016639355.

Sapignoli, Maria, and Ronald Niezen. "Global Legal Institutions." In *The Oxford Handbook of Law and Anthropology*, edited by Marie-Claire Foblets, Mark Goodale, Maria Sapignoli, and Olaf Zenker. Oxford: Oxford University Press, 2021.

Sarat, Austin, and Conor Clarke. "Beyond Discretion: Prosecution, the Logic of Sovereignty, and the Limits of Law." *Law and Social Inquiry* 33, no. 2 (2008): 387–416.

Sarat, Austin, and William L. F. Felstiner. *Divorce Lawyers and Their Clients: Power and Meaning in the Legal Process*. Oxford: Oxford University Press, 1997.

———. "Lawyers and Legal Consciousness: Law Talk in the Divorce Lawyer's Office." *Yale Law Journal* 98, no. 8 (1989): 1663–88.

———. "Legal Realism in Lawyer-Client Communication." In *Language in the Judicial Process*, edited by Judith N. Levi and Anne Graffam Walker, 133–51. New York: Springer, 1990.

Scheppele, Kim Lane. 1990. "Facing Facts in Legal Interpretation." *Representations*, no. 30 (April): 42–77. doi:10.2307/2928446.

Scherr, Caitlyn. "Chasing Democracy: The Development and Acceptance of Jury Trials in Argentina." *University of Miami Inter-American Law Review* 47, no. 2 (2015): 316–53.

Schmitt, Carl. *Political Theology*. Chicago: University of Chicago Press, 1985.

Schwartzberg, Melissa. "Justifying the Jury: Reconciling Justice, Equality, and Democracy, *American Political Science Review* 112, no. 3 (2018): 446–58.

Shapiro, Martin. "On the Regrettable Decline of Law French: Or Shapiro Jettet Le Brickbat." *Yale Law Journal* 90, no. 5 (1981): 1198–204.

Silbey, Susan S. *What the Lower Courts Do: The Work and Role of Courts of Limited Jurisdiction*. Washington, DC: Department of Justice, Federal Justice Research Program, Office for Improvement in the Administration of Justice, 1979.

Silverstein, Michael, and Greg Urban, eds. *Natural Histories of Discourse*. Chicago: University of Chicago Press, 1996.

Simon-Kerr, Julia. "Credibility by Proxy." *George Washington Law Review* 85 (2017): 152–225.

———. "Unchaste and Incredible: The Use of Gendered Conceptions of Honor in Impeachment." *Yale Law Journal* 117, no. 8 (2008): 1854–98.

———. "Uncovering Credibility." In *The Oxford Handbook of Law and Humanities*, edited by Simon Stern, Maksymillan Del Mar, and Bernadette Meyler, 583–600. Oxford: Oxford University Press, 2020.

———. "Unmasking Demeanor." *George Washington Law Review* 88, no. 2 (2020): 158–74.

Smith, Abbe. "'Nice Work If You Can Get It': 'Ethical' Jury Selection in Criminal Defense." *Fordham Law Review* 67 (1998): 523–68.

Smith, Adam. *The Theory of Moral Sentiments*. Edited by Dugald Stewart. 1759. London: Printed for H. G. Bohn, 1853.

Sommers, Samuel R. "On Racial Diversity and Group Decision Making: Identifying Multiple Effects of Racial Composition on Jury Deliberations." *Journal of Personality and Social Psychology* 90, no. 4 (2006): 597–612. https://doi.org/10.1037/0022-3514.90.4.597.

Southworth, Ann, and Catherine Fisk. *The Legal Profession: Ethics in Contemporary Practice*. St. Paul, MN: West Academic Publishing, 2014.

Spears, Jeffrey W., and Cassia C. Spohn. "The Genuine Victim and Prosecutors' Charging Decisions in Sexual Assault Cases." *American Journal of Criminal Justice* 20, no. 2 (1996): 183–205.

Stark, Laura. "Meetings by the Minute(s): How Documents Create Decisions for Institutional Review Boards." In *Social Knowledge in the Making*, edited by Charles Camic, Neil Gross, and Michèle Lamont, 233–56. Chicago: University of Chicago Press, 2011.

Strathern, Marilyn. *The Gender of the Gift: Problems with Women and Problems with Society in Melanesia*. Berkeley: University of California Press, 1988.

Taslitz, Andrew E. "A Feminist Approach to Social Scientific Evidence Foundations." *Michigan Journal of Gender and Law* 5 (1998): 1, 36–37.

———. *Rape and the Culture of the Courtroom*. New York: New York University Press, 1999.

Tetlow, Tania. "Discriminatory Acquittal." *William and Mary Bill of Rights Journal* 18, no. 1 (2009): 75–129.

———. "Granting Prosecutors Constitutional Rights to Combat Discrimination." *University of Pennsylvania Journal of Constitutional Law* 14 (2012): 1117–59.

Thusi, I. India "The Pathological Whiteness of Prosecution." *California Law Review* (forthcoming June 2022).

Tiersma, Peter Meijes. *Legal Language*. Chicago: University of Chicago Press, 1999.

Trivedi, Somil, and Nicole Gonzalez Van Cleve. "To Serve and Protect Each Other: How Police-Prosecutor Codependence Enables Police Misconduct." *Boston University Law Review* 100 (2020): 895–933. www.bu.edu.

Turner, Jenia Iontcheva. "Transparency in Plea Bargaining." *Notre Dame Law Review* 96, no. 1 (2020): 973–1023.

Ugelvik, Thomas. "The Rapist and the Proper Criminal: The Exclusion of Immoral Others as Narrative Work on the Self." In *Narrative Criminology: Understanding Stories of Crime*, edited by Lois Presser and Sveinung Sandberg, 23–41. New York: New York University Press, 2015.

US Courts. Federal Judicial Caseload Statistics, 2020. www.uscourts.gov.

US Courts. Judicial Facts and Figures, 2018 www.uscourts.gov.

Van Cleve, Nicole Gonzalez. *Crook County: Racism and Injustice in America's Largest Criminal Court*. Stanford, CA: Stanford University Press, 2016.

Vidmar, Neil and Hans, Valerie P. *American Juries: The Verdict*. Prometheus Books, 2007.

Vidmar, Neil, ed. *World Jury Systems*. Oxford: Oxford University Press, 2000.

Vitiello, Michael. "Defining the Reasonable Person in the Criminal Law: Fighting the Lernaean Hydra." *Lewis and Clark Law Review* 14, no. 4 (2010): 1435–54. https://law.lclark.edu.

Washington Courts. "GR 37 Jury Selection." General Rules. Adopted April 24, 2018. www.courts.wa.gov.

Weinberg, Steve. "Harmful Error: How Prosecutors Cause Wrongful Convictions." *Journal of the Institute of Justice and International Studies* 7 (2007): 28–31.

Weissenberger, Glen. "Making Sense of Extrinsic Act Evidence: F.R.E. 404(b)." 70 *Iowa Law Review* (1985): 579–614.

Wilf, Eitan. "Rituals of Creativity: Tradition, Modernity, and the 'Acoustic Unconscious' in a U.S. Collegiate Jazz Music Program." *American Anthropologist* 114, no. 1 (2012): 32–44. doi:10.1111/j.1548-1433.2011.01395.x.

Wilson, Richard Ashby. *Incitement on Trial: Prosecuting International Speech Crimes*. Cambridge: Cambridge University Press, 2017.

———. *Writing History in International Criminal Trials*. Cambridge: Cambridge University Press, 2011.

Wright, Ronald F., Kami Chavis, and Gregory Scott Parks. "The Jury Sunshine Project: Jury Selection Data as a Political Issue." *University of Illinois Law Review* 2018, no. 4 (2018): 1407–42.

Wright, Ronald F., and Kay L. Levine. "The Cure for Young Prosecutors' Syndrome." *Arizona Law Review* 56 (2014): 1065–128.

Yaroshefsky, Ellen, and Bruce Green. "Prosecutors' Ethics in Context: Influences on Prosecutorial Disclosure." In *Lawyers in Practice: Ethical Decision Making in Context*, edited by Leslie C. Levin and Lynn M. Mather, 269–92. Chicago: University of Chicago Press, 2012.

Yerkovich, Sally. "Gossiping as a Way of Speaking." *Journal of Communication* 27, no. 1 (1977): 192–96.

Yngvesson, Barbara. *Virtuous Citizens, Disruptive Subjects: Order and Complaint in a New England Court*. New York: Routledge, 1993.

Yung, Corey Rayburn. "How to Lie with Rape Statistics: America's Hidden Rape Crisis." *Iowa Law Review* 99, no. 3 (2014): 1197–236.

Zalman, Marvin, and Olga Tsoudis. "Plucking Weeds from the Garden: Lawyers Speak about Voir Dire." *Wayne Law Review* 51 (Spring 2005): 163–428.

CASES

Batson v. Kentucky, 476 U.S. 79 (1986).

Berger v. United States, 295 U.S. 78, 88 (1934).

Brady v. Maryland, 373 U.S. 83, 87 (1963).

Commonwealth v. Williams, 116 N.E.3d 609, 481 Mass. 443 (Mass., 2019).

Dennis Hall et al. v. Valeska, complaint, 2011. M.D. Ala.

Edmonson v. Leesville Concrete Company, 500 U.S. 614 (1991).

Flowers v. Mississippi, 588 U.S. 139 (2019).

Foster v. Chatman, 578 U.S. ___ (2016).

Foster v. State, 258 Ga. 736, 736, 374 S.E.2d 188, 190 (1988).

Hamling v. United States, 418 U.S. 87, 140, 94 S. Ct. 2887, 2919, 41 L. Ed. 2d 590 (1974).

Hernandez v. New York, 500 U.S. 352, 358, 111 S. Ct. 1859, 1866, 114 L. Ed. 2d 395 (1991).

Georgia v. McCollum, 505 U.S. 42 (1992).

Giglio v. United States, 405 U.S. 150 (1972).

J.E.B. v. Alabama ex rel. T. B. (1994).

Pena-Rodriguez v. Colorado, 137 S. Ct. 855 (2017).

People v. Mickey, 818 P.2d 84 (1991).

People v. Sánchez, 63 Cal. 4th 411, 437, 375 P.3d 812, 837 (2016).

People v. Smith, 417 P.3d 662, 681 (Cal. 2018).

People v. Thomas, 141 Misc. 2d 182, 183, 533 N.Y.S.2d 192, 193 (Sup. Ct. 1988).

Peters v. Kiff, 407 U.S. 493 (1972).

Powers v. Ohio, 499 U.S. 400, 407 (1991).

Rosales-Lopez v. United States, 451 U.S. 182, 188, 101 S. Ct. 1629, 1634, 68 L. Ed. 2d 22 (1981).

Smithkline Beecham Corporation v. Abbott Laboratories. 2014. US Court of Appeals, Ninth Circuit.

Sparf v. United States, 156 U.S. 51, 73–74 (1895).

Sorter v. Austen, 221 Ala. 481, 129 So. 51 (1930).

U.S. v. Battiste, 24 F. Cas. 1042, 1043 (C.C.D. Mass. 1835) (No. 14,545).

U.S. v. Gonzalez, 214 F.3d 1109 (9th Cir. 2000).

INDEX

acquittal: Rule 29 for, 21; witness credibility and, 37–38
Adelswärd, Viveka, 145n17
After Virtue (MacIntyre), 51
ambiguous evidence, 67
American Anthropological Association, 10
Amietta, Santiago Abel, 134n19
analogies, in opening statements, 53–54
antidiscrimination laws, 14, 126; *Batson v. Kentucky* and, 71, 73, 141n2; jury selection and, 72
appellate court, homicide case in, 111–12
Argentina, 150n56
Aristotle, 88
The Art of Rhetoric (Aristotle), 88
assault cases: homicide case as, 105–12; jury trial for, 103–4. *See also* sexual assault cases
"Assessments and the Construction of Context" (Goodwin, C., and Goodwin, M.), 144n1
assistant US attorneys (AUSAs). *See* prosecutors

bank robbery case, 81
Barrera, Leticia, 29
Bashkow, Ira, 119
Batson challenges, 71, 73–83, 87, 126, 141n2
Batson v. Kentucky, 71, 73, 141n2
Baughman, Shima Baradaran, 134n20
Berger, Peter L., 140n9
Berger v. United States, 48, 137n20
Bharara, Preet, 24, 142n8
Bill of Rights, 113

Black Lives Matter, 18
Brady violations, 28
Brady v. Maryland, 138n42
Brenneis, Donald, 118
bribery cases, 35–36; evidence in, 61; opening statements in, 56, 62; surveillance evidence in, 49–50
briefs, 57, 114
Brunnegger, Sandra, 139n1, 146n10
Buell, John, 144n2
Burns, Robert, 114
busted panel (venire loss), 84

capital punishment, fairness of, 3
carjacking cases, 60, 71
car theft cases, 61–62
cause challenge, in jury selection dismissal, 72, 84–85
Chakravarti, Sonali, 150n57
character, 88–102; conflicts of loyalty and, 99–100; of cooperating witnesses, 96; in corruption cases, 102; of defendant, 100–102, 105–12; in fraud cases, 101–2; in homicide case, 105–12; imagined jurors and, 88–89, 99–100, 114; in jury selection, 88–93; race and, 100–102; in sexual assault cases, 101; socioeconomic status and, 100–102; of victims, 97–99; in white-collar crime cases, 101; of witnesses, 93–102, 108–10
character evidence, 89–93, 144n2
child abuse cases, 55, 64, 139n58
childcare commitments, jury selection dismissal for, 85

child pornography cases, 41, 58

class: antidiscrimination laws and, 14; *Batson* challenge for, 83–84; guilty pleas and, 27; imagined jurors and, 2; jury selection dismissal by, 83–84, 87. *See also* socioeconomic status

closing statements, 13; articulating story in, 58–65; imagined jurors and, 53–55; preparation of, 14–15, 51, 52–53; revision of, 15

Collateral Knowledge (Riles), 133n11

Collins, Jennifer, 139n58

color-blind racism, 6

common law, on character evidence, 89–90

common sense, 60; in fraud cases, 66; in homicide case, 107

compassion. *See* sympathy

confessions, 67

Conley, John, 97

"The Conscience of a Prosecutor" (Luban), 17

cooperating witnesses: character of, 96; as liars, 96; overzealous prosecutors and, 66–67; prosecutors and, 37–38; as unindicted coconspirators, 96

Cormack, Bradin, 146n9

corroborating evidence, 59, 64–65

corruption cases, 7; character in, 102; of law enforcement agents, 99–100

court clerks, 6, 117

Coutin, Susan Bibler, 6

credibility: character evidence and, 89–93; conflicts of loyalty and, 99–100; imagined jurors and, 99–100, 114; of law enforcement agents, 35–38; of prosecutors, 75; of victims, 97–99; of witnesses, 14, 15, 37–39, 47, 64–65, 110; of women, 27–28

"Crime and Parenthood" (Collins), 139n58

cross-examination, 13; of defendant, 95; of witnesses, 5, 52

declined cases: absence of public disclosure in, 19; for drug cases, 115; ethics of, 20; imagined jurors and, 2; in *Justice Manual*, 20; for misdemeanors, 25; percentage of, 18; power in, 25; public perception of, 20

defendants: character evidence on, 89–91; character of, 100–102, 105–12; confession of, 67; credibility of, 15; cross-examination of, 95; descriptive language about, 61–62; as first-time offenders, 145n17; in fraud cases, 45, 48, 51–52; in gang cases, 45; in homicide case, 105–12; imagined jurors and, 115; indictment of, 34; intelligibility of evidence and, 58; juror gender and, 81–82; as liars, 94–95; mercy for, 31; people of color as, 122; plea agreements and, 45–46; race of, 6, 100–102; sentencing guidelines and, 27; socioeconomic status of, 100–102; sympathy for, 39–41

"Defendants' Interpretations of Encouragements in Court" (Adelswärd), 145n17

defense attorneys: cause challenges and, 85; ethics of, 12; in homicide case, 106; judges and, 138n36; sentences and, 138n36; victim character and, 97–98; witness character and, 93–94

democracy, 11

Department of Homeland Security, 57–58

Department of Justice, 18–19, 26, 42

direct examination, 37, 106–7

discursive strategies, 6

Divorce Lawyers and Their Clients (Sarat and Felstiner), 147n28

DNA evidence, 55, 64

drug cases, 45; declined cases for, 115; evidence intelligibility in, 56–57; jury appeal and, 36, 44; prosecutorial discretion in, 17–18, 31; socioeconomic status and, 100–102

race in, 75–87, 126; race neutrality in, 74–75, 87; racism in, 15; religious affiliation in, 76, 100; sidebar in, 12, 84
jury selection dismissals, 76, 78; cause challenge in, 84–85; character evidence in, 91–92; for financial hardship, 84, 85, 86, 124; of jurors of color, 122; peremptory strikes for, 8, 77, 83, 86; race and, 8; in sexual assault cases, 92; socioeconomic status and, 8; victims in, 91. *See also Batson* challenges
"Jury's Rise as Lie Detector" (Fisher), 150n50
jury testing, 40
jury trials: for assault case, 103–4; *Batson* challenges and, 71; declining numbers of, 1, 28–32, 50, 133n3; guilty verdict in, 124; for homicide case, 105–12; imagined jurors and, 114; juror compensation in, 124–25; in Norway, 126–27; prosecutorial discretion and, 28–32; rarity of, 14; reimagining system for, 123–28; right to, 34. *See also* judges; judicial discretion
justice: conceptions of, 58–65, 139n1; imagined jurors and, 4, 15–16, 48–49, 115; judges and, 139n2; proof and, 5; prosecutors and, 14, 24, 26, 48–49, 58–65, 119
Justice Manual, 18–19, 20

Keane, Webb, 103
kickbacks, 62
Kohler-Hausmann, Issa, 135n24

Latour, Bruno, 12
Law as Culture (Rosen), 113
law enforcement agents: character evidence and, 91; corruption cases of, 99–100; credibility of, 38; drug cases and, 44; imagined jurors and, 21; jury selection and, 82, 91–92, 93; overzealous surveillance by, 43; political affili-

ation and, 99–100; transparency of, 11; undercover, 44
legal language, 136n12; analyses of, 116; for prosecutorial discretion, 23; translation of, 56
liars: character evidence and, 89; defendants as, 94–95; in homicide case, 107; witnesses as, 94, 95–96, 102
"Liars! Cheaters! Evildoers! (De Luca and Buell), 144n2
Local Knowledge (Geertz), 136n19
Luban, David, 17
De Luca, Tom, 144n2
Luckman, Thomas, 140n9

MacIntyre, Alasdair, 51
Markel, Dan, 31
Marshall, Thurgood, 70
Matoesian, Gregory, 97–98
McGranahan, Carole, 90
mercy, for defendants, 31
Mertz, Elizabeth, 133n11
Misdemeanorland (Kohler-Hausmann), 135n24
misdemeanors, 27, 30; declined cases for, 25
mistrial, in homicide case, 107
Murder and the Reasonable Man (Lee), 141n4
Murray, Bill, 107–8
Murray, Kerrel, 134n20

Nader, Laura, 11
narrative: challenges during trial, 106–7; ethnography and, 116–18; formulating justice through, 58–65; judge and, 110–11; legal technique of, 5–8; negotiating witness credibility through, 94–95, 98, 101–2; opening statements as, 51–53; prosecutors as creators of, 53–55; translating the law through, 55–58
Natapoff, Alexandra, 25, 27, 137n26, 139n55
National Center for State Courts, 124–25

ABOUT THE AUTHOR

ANNA OFFIT is Assistant Professor of Law at the Dedman School of Law and Assistant Professor of Anthropology (by courtesy) at the Dedman College of Humanities and Sciences at Southern Methodist University. She holds a PhD in Anthropology from Princeton University, an MPhil in Social Anthropological Analysis from the University of Cambridge, and a JD from the Georgetown University Law Center. Her empirical legal research has been supported by the National Science Foundation and the Fulbright Foundation.

Made in the USA
Middletown, DE
25 July 2024

57954109R00117